MOLIÈRE

SCHOOL FOR WIVES

L'École des Femmes

AN ADAPTATION IN RHYMED VERSE

BY ERIC M. STEEL

Modern Language Department
State University College
at Brockport, New York

BARRON'S EDUCATIONAL SERIES, INC.

WOODBURY, NEW YORK

INTRODUCTION

PART I

The Author

The Sun King, Louis XIV, so the story goes, asked the renowned critic, Boileau, to name the greatest writer of the age. "Molière, sire," replied Boileau. "I would not have thought so," said the king. "But no doubt you know better than I." One is prone to wonder whom Louis expected Boileau to name. Probably Corneille or Racine, the justly famous authors of tragedies which lent as much luster to Louis's reign as the splendor of Versailles. After all, Molière excelled only in comedy and farce. Besides, he was an actor as well as a playwright and thus ineligible even for Christian burial. To make matters worse, he acted in his own farces, and so failed to make the French Academy, although the members of this august body were so impressed by his genius that their regret was deep when Molière's refusal to stop acting in farces prevented them from making him one of them. Posterity has more than confirmed Boileau's judgment. The consensus today is that he is the greatest name in the history of French literature, as well as the greatest writer of high comedy of all time.

A biographical sketch of Molière must be liberally sprinkled with such reservations as "so the story goes" and equivalent phrases. Information about several phases of his life is scanty and often contradictory, since Molière's activities aroused bitter controversy in his lifetime and since modern critics not only have also disagreed on the validity of evidence produced throughout the years but have interpreted this evidence differently.

Born Jean Baptiste Poquelin in Paris in 1622, he is alleged to have taken the name of Molière from a village of that name in which he played in his struggling early days. His father was an upholsterer patronized by the king and both he, and later his son, were appointed the king's "valet tapissier" and as such were responsible to some extent for the king's material comfort both in Paris and in the provinces. It is presumably as a member of the king's retinue that he traveled to Provence in 1642 and there met and fell in love with Madeleine Béjart, who with her brother and sisters belonged to a troop of actors who happened to be playing in a small town in the area at the time when Molière was passing through.

Before his meeting with Madeleine, he had studied for almost five years, from 1636 to 1641, at the renowned Jesuit college of Clermont in Paris, where he saw plays performed even if he did not act in them himself. At any rate, there is a strong probability that his grandfather took him to see the farces staged at the Hôtel de Bourgogne, which was later to be one of the two theatres with which

Molière had to compete for both royal and popular favor. In 1641, the free-thinking philosopher Gassendi came to teach in Paris. Molière and Cyrano de Bergerac were his two most famous pupils. His contact with Gassendi and his readings in philosophy directed by his teacher seem to have left an indelible imprint on his mind. At any rate, it was at this time that he embarked on a translation of *De Rerum Natura*, a six-volume poem in which the Latin poet Lucretius expounded the atomic philosophy of Epicurus and at the same time fulminated against the Roman *religio*, which he equated with superstition. Molière's enthusiasm for Lucretius's views prompted him to undertake a verse translation of his poem. It is unlikely that his passion for Lucretius, which provided the incentive necessary to undertake an enterprise of such magnitude, could ever have deserted him in later life, when he took an even dimmer view of the *religio* which he saw manifested around him. At any rate, not only his profession but his philosophy were anathema to the clergy, and the only pious act we know of his having committed (apart from his marriage and the baptism of his children) was his presence at communion the year before he died, conceivably in the hope of being granted a decent burial. Madeleine Béjart, with the same aim in mind, also communed with him and again on her deathbed. In addition, she took the apparently essential step, which does not seem even to have occurred to Molière, of renouncing her theatrical profession.

Before taking to the stage, Molière studied law and apparently made some attempt to fit into his father's business. Soon, however, whether or not under the influence of Madeleine Béjart, he formed with her and with her brother and sisters a nondescript troop, rented a tennis court and launched the Illustre Théâtre. It was unfortunately located in the parish of a priest called Olier, who promptly sent the actors packing. Several other tennis courts served as equally wretched stages, but the company's success was so limited that Molière got arrested for being unable to pay the bills for the most rudimentary stage equipment: tapestries in the rear, curtains at the sides through which the actors struggled to make their exits and their entrances, and a few candles for illumination. The dim lighting had one advantage at least, as Louis Jouvet found when he tried to stage *Don Juan* for an audience accustomed to 500 times more candlepower than was common in the 17th century. It was relatively easy for Molière to send Don Juan convincingly down to hell through a trapdoor on a stage where, even in a "normal" play, nobody in the audience had a very clear idea of what was going on!

Soon Molière was forced to forsake Paris for the provinces, where he traveled for twelve years. It was in Lyons that he presented his first original (or semi-original) farce, *L'Étourdi*, inspired by, if not wholly copied from, an Italian play. Where plot was concerned, Molière prided himself no more on originality than did Shakespeare. As he said, he took his material where he found it, and he found it in the Latin plays of Plautus and Terence, in the Italian *commedia dell'arte*, and occasionally in the plays of Frenchmen such as Scarron and his fellow student, Cyrano. In 1654, he won the rather stingy patronage of the Prince de Conti, a brilliant but corrupt young nobleman, who shortly, however, "got religion," foreswore the theatre, and persecuted Molière more vigorously than he had ever sponsored him. Righteously indignant, Molière is alleged to have used the prince as a model for his Don Juan, whom he described as a "vicious nobleman."

In 1653, Molière won the favor of Monsieur, brother of the king, and for the first time Molière had a royal audience. The story of Molière's relationship with Louis XIV is one with two sides, on both of which much can be said. The king has been called a "firm friend" of Molière's, and unquestionably for several years Louis acted as Molière's generous patron, finding him theatres, first in the Petit Bourbon then in the Palais Royal, allowing himself to be entertained regularly by Molière's plays, conversing often as much as two hours a day with him, conferring upon him pensions and gifts, acting as godfather to his son. But it is also incontestable that Louis was not always a friend in need. After allegedly persuading Molière to write *Tartuffe* in order to bait the bigots, Louis ordered the play stopped and refused for five years, to Molière's dismay, to allow a watered-down version of it to be publicly performed. The evidence is strong that

Louis—inexplicably—lost interest in Molière. How else could he have granted Molière's friend and collaborator, the musician Lulli, the sole right to use ballet music in spite of the fact that Molière had delighted the king with so many successful ballets—and followed this insult up with the injury of cutting all producers except Lulli down to six singers and twelve violins? Louis does appear to have made a half-hearted effort to get his former protégé decently buried. The story—probably apocryphal—is that Louis asked the parish priest of St. Eustache how far down the ground was holy. "Four feet, sire," replied the priest. "Then put him down six and be done with it!" said the king. Whether this be true or false, the fact is that Molière was consigned under cover of darkness to a section of the cemetery reserved for suicides and unchristened children. Whereas Louis's obligation as a statesman may have regretfully obliged him to do less for Molière than he would have liked, we have no record of his being remorseful for such unkindnesses as refusing to see Molière after he had driven out in ill health from Paris to St. Germain on a cold day. It is probable that Louis, who cannot have helped being grateful for the entertainment afforded him, considered him as he considered the soldiers whom he sent, no doubt regretfully, to die in Flanders—as expendable. Unlike Voltaire, who accused Frederick the Great of having squeezed the orange and then thrown it away, Molière registered no complaint, but this may be simply because he was less capable of resentment than Voltaire.

Even more brisk is the three-hundred-year-old controversy over the identity of Molière's wife, née Armande Béjart. She was definitely either the sister or the daughter of Madeleine Béjart, whose friendship with Molière had stood the test of 20 years when he married Armande.

It is significant that all of Molière's contemporaries apparently believed Armande to be the daughter of Madeleine; his enemies clamoring that he himself was the father; his friends, including Louis XIV, believing her to be the daughter of another of Madeleine's lovers, probably the Count Esprit de Modène, whose mistress Madeleine was when she met Molière and to whom she seems to have occasionally reverted. In the 19th century documents came to light which some scholars have construed as proof that Armande was the sister of Madeleine. It is perhaps coincidental that this interpretation should have been given in an age which was more sensitive to scandal than either the 17th or the 20th centuries. Even today, however, the author of the *Encyclopedia Britannica* article on Molière clings to the theory that Armande and Madeleine were sisters and rejects the others as "foul calumnies" which he regrets to see "supported in the essays of modern French critics." It is possibly for this reason that the *Encyclopedia Britannica* article does not mention a biography of Molière dating later than 1880. It is impossible in this limited space to present even a fraction of the evidence. Suffice it to say that this writer leans towards the view of the "modern critics" that Armande was Madeleine's but not Molière's daughter. Those desirous of reviewing the evidence should read both the *Britannica* article and pages 115-116 and 124-126 of Jean Meyer's *Molière*.

What is of infinitely greater concern to the student of Molière is the nature of the relationship between him and his wife. Armande, though not a raving beauty, was a most attractive woman, a talented actress and singer, and the probability is strong that she was dazzled by the genius and prestige of her suitor. She saw her marriage as a means of furthering her theatrical ambitions. No critic— not even a nineteenth-century critic—has contended that she loved Molière. He loved her to distraction. His devotion to her was the tragic flaw that may well have helped bring him to a premature grave. He seems to have suffered less from her alleged infidelities than from her invincible indifference. Though in his *Critique of the School For Wives* Molière insists that he portrayed, not individuals, but types, it may be legitimately assumed that he drew more freely from some examples of the type than from others. At any rate, the ferocious coquette Celimène in *The Misanthrope* comes very close to what we know about Armande. The friction between them cannot wholly, of course, be ascribed to her. If Molière had had the time to give her the adulation she seems to have required, the rough marital path they trod together would doubtless have been smoother. As one critic has remarked, if Molière had lived several lives and had devoted one to Armande, their marriage might well have been a happy one. The

consensus is that it was not. And one scholar has gone
so far as to hint darkly that there was an element of
mystery about Molière's death which his wife might have
been the best qualified person to solve.

These conjectural matters over, we can return to our
brief exposé of Molière's life and works. The first play
produced in the Petit Bourbon, which the king assigned
to him, was *Le Dépit Amoureux*. It has been called the best
dramatic work produced in France up to that time, and
it was followed by an even greater success, *Les Précieuses
Ridicules*, wherein for the first time Molière was not
indebted to the stock characters and situations provided
by either Rome or Italy. He ridiculed the affected manners
and conversation which the ladies of the French provinces
had adopted in an attempt to ape the elegance of the
ladies of Paris. Their ultra-refined speech, which not only
prevented them from calling a spade a spade, but com-
pelled them to ignore the very existence of a spade, led
them to perpetrate such atrocities as calling chairs and
teeth "commodities of conversation" and "furnishings of
the mouth" respectively. The success of *Les Précieuses
Ridicules* maddened his rivals, who were jealous of his
success either as playwright or director or both. Two other
theatres, the Hôtel de Bourgogne and the Marais, were
in constant competition with Molière's Palais Royal for
both the royal favor and the accolade of the public. An
abortive attempt at tragedy or tragi-comedy, *Don Garcie
de Navarre*, was sufficient to convince Molière that his

genius lay in comedy and farce. In *School For Husbands*, the plot of which came partly from Terence and partly from Boccaccio, the two main characters are nonetheless contemporary Frenchmen, and the civilized one who embarks on a marriage with his ward 40 years his junior may well have been Molière partly as he was, partly as he wanted to be. After his marriage to Armande in February 1662 came *School For Wives*, of which more will be said in the second part of this preface. The furious attack it provoked both on himself and his play stung Molière to retaliate, and his ridicule reduced his enemies to not wholly impotent rage, because the charges of blasphemy and irreverence they leveled at him stuck. After another comedy, *Le Mariage Forcé*, Molière, rashly considering offence the best method of defence, painted a perfect portrait of the religious hypocrite in *Tartuffe*, and was, of course, accused of ridiculing "true" religion. In the mêlée, as has been mentioned, Louis did not come to the rescue. Whether the clergy was so powerful that to champion Molière would have been poor statesmanship is a debatable question. Although Louis allowed the play to be prohibited, Molière's company was nonetheless officially called the "troupe du roi."

The popular success in 1665 of *Don Juan* was tremendous, but so was the clerical condemnation of the play, which allegedly preached atheism, and Molière did not wait for it to be banned. He withdrew it himself after 15 performances. A light comedy, *Le Docteur Amoureux*, staged in 1666, preceded the play that many have considered his masterpiece, *Le Misanthrope*. At least one of its ideas is that the man who tells nothing but the truth, whether to his friend or to an acquaintance who happens to be an aspiring poet, or to his flirtatious lady love, will soon find himself alone. Molière's attack on the hypocrisy of French society is so scathing, and Alceste, the victim of his own frankness, so admirable in his scorn for the dishonesty he sees around him, that this high comedy comes close indeed to tragedy. To prevent it from becoming so, Molière, a dogged advocate of the common sense which he sometimes lacked himself, had to make Alceste's passion for frankness appear, if not vicious, at least foolish, and therefore ludicrous. Philinte, the exponent of wisdom and moderation who appears in so many of Molière's plays, deplores the excessive character of Alceste's forthrightness, and points out that social intercourse is impossible without the white lie. Much of Molière himself has unquestionably gone into Alceste—his hatred of sham and deceit and, most of all, his jealous passion for Celimène-Armande. Of the two main characters Philinte is certainly the wiser, Alceste the more noble. *Le Misanthrope* enjoyed a great *succès d'estime*, but it is more popular with the theatre-going public today than it was with the audiences of Molière's day.

Around this time the tuberculosis which was to prove fatal set in, yet Molière continued as active as before in all three capacities: author, actor, and producer. Possibly the most fatiguing of his activities was the staging of the comedy ballets which Louis loved, and which forced him to commute feverishly to Versailles, Chambord, St. Germain, or wherever the king happened to be at the time. Among the best works of his last years were *George Dandin*, in which he ridiculed the enriched peasant who foolishly buys a wife above his breeding; *The Miser*, which Balzac, who made a study of avarice, readily admitted was more penetrating than his own *Eugenie Grandet; The Would-Be Gentleman*, probably the most amusing study of the parvenu in all literature; *The Learned Ladies*, in which he reverts to a theme similar to that of the *Les Précieuses Ridicules* and mocks, if not learning itself, at least the pretentious display of learning in women. Molière, like the more enlightened of his contemporaries, placed little faith in the medical men of his day, and their inevitable inability to cure him made his final play, *The Imaginary Invalid*, the most devastating satire of the medical profession until perhaps Jules Romains's no less famous *Dr. Knock*. Aggravated by overwork, domestic frustration, the forfeiture of the king's favor, the loss of one of his closest friends, Madeleine Béjart, to death and of some others to estrangement, Molière's ill health took a turn for the worse in the August of 1672. On the 7th he could not appear, and the comedy billed for that night was canceled. In October his only son died. In November he began working on the production of the *Imaginary Invalid*. The first performance was on February 10, 1673 and on the 17th, a year to the day after the death of Madeleine, he was stricken by what is described none too convincingly as a cough, which burst a blood vessel. He died an hour and three quarters later. None of the priests summoned by his wife consented to come to his bedside, and he was given a nocturnal and indecent burial by the clergy of St. Eustache.

Even in his youth, Molière, who was well built, moderately good-looking, energetic and animated, wore an air of gravity which intensified under the strain of the burdens he was called upon to bear, and in his latter years he was notoriously morose and melancholy. Fortunately, his sense of humor never deserted him as a playwright and his thick lips, large mouth and nose contributed to rendering him an admirable interpreter of all his own comic roles.

His genius made him a fascinating conversationalist, and his native goodness a lovable friend. All but the most worthless of his colleagues and associates idolized him and, to his credit, his enemies hated him "with a perfect hatred." When he became estranged from men of merit like Racine and the musician Lulli, the fault was theirs, not his. The only questionable act in his entire career may have been his marriage with Armande Béjart after 20 years of friendship with her mother. If the defenders of Molière are to be trusted, however, for many years prior to the marriage Madeleine and he had been no more than friends. It is also alleged that Madeleine favored the match and that Armande was bent on marrying the man who seemed most likely to be able to satisfy her ambition.

The only other weakness—if it can be called one—with which he might be reproached is the irascibility he developed eventually towards Armande, who seems to have taken an almost sadistic pleasure in harassing him similar to that of which the hero of Somerset Maugham's *Of Human Bondage* was the victim.

One of his literary rivals, De Visé, called him a dangerous man because he never went anywhere without his eyes and his ears wide open. De Visé went so far as to affirm that, like Pickering in Shaw's *Pygmalion*, he carried a notebook in which he recorded all he saw and read. This capacity for meticulous observation, plus the fact that he had traveled throughout France and was as much at home at court as in a tavern, is responsible for both the scope and the authenticity of his portrait gallery, ranging as it does from courtiers with their fine ladies, upper and middle class burghers and their wives, doctors, merchants, trademen, peasants, valets and lady's maids, plus an assortment of rogues, rascals, and fools on every social level.

Since Molière started out as a writer of farce and continued to inject farce into most of his so-called high comedies, many of his portraits were overdrawn, and some of them are downright caricatures, like those of Charles Dickens. The exaggeration is generally, however, not a distortion but an intensification of the truth. By not contenting himself with rendering the mere surface reality, but by penetrating instead to the very soul of the character, Molière was an unconscious pioneer of expressionism.

Even in his farces, Molière constantly affirmed that his purpose was to instruct as well as to amuse. It is pertinent, therefore, to inquire as to the nature of the morality he preached. Undoubtedly it was not the Christian ethic expounded by Sts. Paul and Augustine, and by Molière's contemporary, John Bunyan, in his *Pilgrim's Progress*. Unlike the Christian moralists, Molière espoused both the world and the flesh—eschewing only the devil. For him as for Rabelais and Montaigne, man was predominantly good, and this makes him a precursor of Rousseau. But, like Voltaire, he also believed, though perhaps not so fervently, that society was likewise good. Even when visited by the gravest doubts about the beneficence of society, as when he wrote *Le Misanthrope*, he faced the fact that it was here to stay, and in each of his masterpieces he introduced a Mr. Worldly Wiseman, whom Bunyan depicted as a snare in the path of the upright, but whom Molière extolled as a promoter of the compromise which is essential if society is to run smoothly.

While believing in the inherent goodness of human nature, Molière fully realized that it occasionally produced "sports"—misers like Harpagon, dolts like Orgon, tyrants like Arnolphe, connivers like Tartuffe. Molière's prime purpose was to show "what fools these mortals are." He realized that their folly, when viewed with a less indulgent eye, can readily pass for vice and can have tragic consequences to the people exposed to it. But he always paused, sometimes on the very brink of the tragedy he could have written had he wished. What gave him pause? Possibly a quirk in character similar to that to which George Bernard Shaw has confessed—an irresistible urge to jest even when he felt most serious. The buffoon in Shaw —and possibly in Molière—was in constant contention with the philosopher and the potential writer of tragedies.

The sole antidote that Molière prescribes for the man who is psychically sick—and really the only one available in those pre-Freudian days—was a liberal dose of reason. Those whose nature prompts them to do evil to their fellowmen must listen—or be made to listen—to the voice of reason. Happiness will thus accrue to both the natural and the social man who so behaves. Euphoria in a fool's paradise is, of course, hardly Molière's ideal. His discourse with Gassendi and Lucretius convinced him that the pursuit of truth is the greatest of all the virtues, whether it ends in joy or sorrow. Throughout his life hechampioned the cause of truth, honesty, freedom of inquiry and expression, and he suffered the consequences. It can only be because of the afore-mentioned quirk in his character that in the play where he created a character identical to himself in this respect, Alceste in *The Misanthrope*, and could have made him the hero of a great tragedy, he shrugged his shoulders and abandoned him to the ridicule of the audience.

Molière's place in the international Hall of Fame is, of course, debatable. The fact that he has been called the grand master of French literature inevitably suggests a comparison with another actor, author, producer, who is the most eminent figure in English literature. A piquant parallel between Molière and Shakespeare has been drawn by a French critic, who observes that both men took to the stage at the age of 21, toured the provinces for 12 years before producing a play, wrote 33 plays, and died in their fifty-second year. As a writer, Shakespeare far surpassed Molière in scope, since the latter did not write the tragedies of which he was capable. If, however, we base our view, as we must, on the imperfect knowledge we possess of the life of both, Molière towers over Shakespeare as a man— for the same reason that Shaw contended he too was greater than Shakespeare. Shakespeare made his edifying characters deliver themselves of edifying speeches, but he was content to hold up a mirror to the world around him, and we do not hear of him launching even a feeble protest against the Establishment of his day. Both Molière and Shaw, on the other hand, sought to leave the world a better place to live in, and they made sacrifices for their convictions. What Sainte–Beuve has said of Molière can not be said of Shakespeare: "To love Molière is to be cured forever of fanaticism, intolerance, harshness of any sort... it is to be immune to cold, cruel, political and puritanical hatreds and spites... it is to be poles apart, likewise, from those who are indifferent to such horrors perpetrated around them."

The best epitaph for Molière may well be Horatio's verdict on Hamlet: *We shall not look upon his like again.*

INTRODUCTION

PART TWO

The Play

School for Wives was not only the smash hit of Molière's entire career. It was also his first attempt at high comedy or, as it has been called, intermediate comedy, a genre intended to bridge the gap between comedy-farce and tragedy. Notwithstanding, a few brief scenes of the farce which Molière loved have contrived to intrude. These, in the opinion of this writer at least, add to rather than detract from the sheer delight the play affords. The title is somewhat misleading. *School for Husbands* would have been more appropriate, and Molière might have called it that had he not quite recently written a play by that name.

What prompted Molière to write *School for Wives?* The target he aimed at in all his plays has been discussed in an earlier part of this preface. Dorante, his spokesman in the playlet he wrote in defense of *School*, says bluntly: "I'm on the side of common sense." Molière has proclaimed his purpose more specifically: "to show that there is a sort of natural balance in society and that the selfishness of man cannot, no matter what precautions he takes, stifle the legitimate independence of woman." What circumstances if any in Molière's personal life led him to champion the cause of women? The controversy over whether Molière used his own experiences as material has been brisk and, perhaps, pointless. It indeed would have been surprising if this man who was "all eyes and ears" as he searched for material for his plays in the people around him, had been deaf and blind in his contacts with his wife and in his self-scrutiny. If, as he was preparing to marry Armande Béjart, a girl 21 years his junior, he wrote a play in which a sophisticated older man takes a young woman 40 years his junior in a marriage which promises happiness to both, it would be surprising if he were not whistling to keep his own courage up. If in *School For Wives* he shows how a man 20 years older than his prospective bride should NOT behave if he wants to win her love, is it not probable that he was playing both the teacher and the student, and charting the difficult course he knew he would have to follow himself in his relationship with Armande? If later, in the *Misanthrope*, Alceste is incensed by the coquetry of Célimène with whom he is madly in love, is Molière not both chastising Armande for her vanity and himself for the irascibility that drove her even further from him? Finally, if in the *Learned Ladies*, he reverses himself and contends that whatever a woman's outside interests may be, she had better devote most of her energy to home-making, could this not spring from the wish that Armande, whose ambition to make a hit both on and off the stage drove him to distraction, would follow this sage advice?

In 1662 there were 31 performances of *School For Wives*, 88 before Molière's death, 1200 between 1662 and 1870, although in the 18th century Molière was quite out of fashion. In the twentieth century *School For Wives*, particularly as it was staged by Louis Jouvet, has enjoyed a tremendous vogue, which still continues.

Before speculating on what Molière had to say in *School For Wives*, let us see what he has said. Arnolphe, a prosperous bourgeois convinced that every intelligent woman is bent on deceiving her husband, is bent nonetheless on marrying. His sensible friend Chrysalde—less convinced of the frailty of woman, tries to dissuade Arnolphe, sensing in him the sort of jealous, possessive husband that invites deception. Arnolphe has planned to avert disaster by having chosen as his bride a 4-year-old "orphan" and carefully preserved her ignorance in a nunnery. Today, he assures his friend, "nothing that you have known can match the ignorance of her young mind."

He nonetheless intends to take all reasonable precautions, so he instructs his hillbilly servants to protect her from possible contact with the outside world. Meantime a gay young blade by the name of Horace, son of Arnolphe's best "college" friend, Oronte, comes up from the provinces, eager to see Paris. Arnolphe is eager for him to see it, generously offers him his purse, and promises him (Molière is cruelly adept in his use of dramatic irony) he will have a lively time with the Parisian ladies! "Ah, no," sighs Horace, "I'm in love with a wonderful girl—called Agnes!" "Grrrr!" says Arnolphe, *sotto voce* of course, for if he is to foil his youthful rival he must be cunning. With engaging candor Horace tells Arnolphe what Arnolphe already knows—that Agnes is guarded by a jealous old curmudgeon who plans to keep her for himself. He adds, however, that he and Agnes have enjoyed a balcony scene and that his love is requited. The only problem is outwitting the old curmudgeon. Will Arnolphe help? Seething within, Arnolphe promises his cooperation. Throughout the play Molière exploits to the full the comic possibilities of Horace's ignorance of Arnolphe's identity.

Feverishly Arnolphe questions Agnes, who, with the innocence that he has done everything to foster, tells him all. She loves Horace, she gave him all he asked, and he took from her...... "What?" demands Arnolphe in agony —in a scene which started Molière off on his losing battle with the rigidly righteous of his day. "A ribbon," says Agnes. "High time you were married!" snorts Arnolphe. Agnes is delighted—until she discovers that he, not Horace, is to be the groom. All is not yet lost, thinks Arnolphe. So after preaching a fire-and-brimstone sermon to his ward, he forces her to read the Ten Maxims of Marriage (more trouble for Molière with the Church!) and meditates on further plans for averting disaster. (There is probably, *Oedipus Rex* nothwithstanding, no better example of sustained dramatic irony than *School For Wives* in the history of the theatre. The audience is constantly in the know, while Horace or Arnolphe is constantly in the dark.) The next time Horace attempts to converse with his ladylove, he receives, instead of a loving word, a brick. Arnolphe's spirits soar! But attached to the brick was—a love letter. Arnolphe plummets back into hell! This sudden switch from elation to despair is one of the most comical moments in this uproariously comical play. The letter is a miniature masterpiece—a "simple aveu" by a sensitive, tender, trusting girl. Reading it, Arnolphe grinds his teeth in silent rage. Eventually, however, his anger turns to anguish. He has fallen in love unawares with this girl he planned to treat as a chattel. His only hope now is to marry her without delay and he summons a notary to draw up the contract. (Here follows a short scene of deliciously extravagant farce.) Now an elated Horace enters with the news that in spite of all Arnolphe's precautions, Horace has found his way into Agnes' room, and the artless girl, her wit sharpened by love, coolly hid him in the closet just as the old curmudgeon entered for his tour of inspection. Tonight, Horace obligingly continues to relate, with the aid of a ladder he will again rejoin his beloved. At this point the plot has to thicken, and it does. The half-demented Arnolphe instructs his servants to lie in wait for Horace and strike him down. They do so, not wisely but almost too well. For a moment Arnolphe is terrified that they have killed him, but we in the audience know better. Horace staggers in to announce that as he lay in the proverbial pool of blood, Agnes succoured him and swore she would never leave him. She is at present on his hands, but, fearing for her reputation, Horace asks Arnolphe if he will act as chaperon until they can marry. Indeed Arnolphe will! Miraculously, happy days are here again! (The transfer of Agnes is effected under cover of night in order to make her failure to recognize her guardian as plausible as possible.) The high point in horror is reached when she does recognize him! The sweet girl from the nunnery tries to reason Arnolphe out of his foul intent. When she fails, the outraged woman she has become hurls defiance in his teeth. Arnolphe foams at the mouth and hustles her off in a carriage under armed guard.

But the darkest hour is just before the dawn, and the rest of the play is unmitigated melodrama. Molière has no time to unravel the Gordian knot, so he slices through it with a slash of his sabre. An old friend of Oronte's, Enrique, has just come back from the Americas, naturally with a huge fortune. He has a daughter, and the two old cronies want to cement their friendship by having their children wed. Horace is in despair, and Arnolphe is triumphant—until it turns out that Enrique's daughter (to make a long, implausible story short) is none other than Agnes! The happy ending is enjoyed by all except Arnolphe, who exits, in a state of near-collapse, all his knavish tricks frustrated at last.

The plot is obviously shot through with so many implausibilities that to point them out, let alone reproach Molière for them, is to behave as if his purpose were to produce a mystery or even a well made play, which justly flops if too much strain is imposed on the audience's credulity and if the machinery creaks too audibly. Molière resembled most of his classical compeers in that his sole intent was to study what he believed to be basic human behavior. *School For Wives* would never have been written had he not been convinced that in his day, as in every day before or since, some mature male who passes for normal becomes obsessed with the desire to possess some immature female either in or out of wedlock, profiting as amply as he can from her ignorance and inexperience. It is in his success or failure to make this duel meaningful and on this alone that *School For Wives* must be judged.

Its "defects," loudly publicized by Molière's literary rivals, are no defects at all. He broke the rules, he strewed the play with colloquialisms and referred to vulgar things like cream tarts. He was prone to long speeches that appeared to slow down the action. All these criticisms are founded on fact, but they are "incompetent, immaterial and irrelevant." Molière preserved "the greatest rule of all" inviolate—"to give pleasure," and he recked little of the others. By scrupulously obeying one unity, however—unity of place—he got himself into hot water with a number of modern critics. This rule obliged Molière to pick one place for an action that could plausibly take place only in several. So he picked "a public square" and shrugged his shoulders. Obviously, then, there is nothing to be gained by pointing out that it is curious that when Arnolphe and Horace meet they always happen to be alone ("was there a plague in Paris at the time?") or by expressing surprise that Arnolphe should choose a square rather than a drawing room to lecture Agnes, and the identical square rather than the pantry to dragoon his servants. Enlightened producers have blithely overlooked this "defect" and have built sets featuring house gables and garden alleys of pleasing aspect—and no spectator in his right mind has worried a whit about how the *dramatis personae* happened to get there at all, let alone simultaneously.

Much has been made, too, of the coincidences, which are unquestionably too numerous to be entirely plausible. One critic has observed that Arnolphe has to contend with a veritable army of them and is therefore locked in a struggle not only with his obsession but with Destiny— presumably like Racine's Phaedra, who is presented as fighting a losing battle with the inexorable goddess Venus. So to contend is rather to emulate the naiveté of the readers of Blondie, who mailed in lavish gifts to the newspaper offices when Blondie's creator decided it was time for her to have a baby. Molière, not Destiny, is obviously pulling the strings, and he made carefree and unscrupulous use of coincidence simply to keep the action moving.

His greatest "carelessness" is evident in the dénouement, which, as has been amply pointed out, is sheer melodrama. But Molière could hardly have cared less. Once he had demonstrated the impact of character on character, his task was over. All that remained was to clear the stage as expeditiously as possible. *Tartuffe* and the *Would-Be Nobleman*—to mention only two—also finish with a cock-and-bull tale.

That *School* contains too little action is a slightly more valid criticism. But Molière himself has admirably refuted it by pointing out that the long narrations are really action in disguise. When, for example, Horace tells Arnolphe how he has or has not been making out with Agnes, he does so as vividly as if we were there to see it, and we have the extra dividends of savoring Arnolphe's ill-suppressed fury and watching Horace wade deeper and deeper into trouble with each spicy detail.

Since Molière's overwhelming concern was with the depiction of character, let us try to discover exactly what he sought to depict in Arnolphe and Agnes. Is the protagonist of this play, as has been asked regarding Shylock in *The Merchant of Venice*, a tragic or a comic character? The mere fact that the tragic overtones, though unmistakable, are few and far between provides an easy answer: Arnolphe is not a tragic character. True, he suffers all the agonies of the damned and his ordeal is almost equal to that of Othello, but Molière is careful to avoid evoking pity or terror on Arnolphe's behalf by employing two devices. He makes Arnolphe talk far too much about his anguish, and as a result we incline to get bored rather than compassionate. Also, each of his moments of agony is followed either by something in the nature of a wisecrack or a comic interlude which brings the near-tragedy down to earth like a deflated balloon. Yet neither is Arnolphe a wholly ludicrous character. He does not resemble, as has been suggested, the clown in the slapstick comedy, whose "sufferings" amuse us more the more intense they get. We know the slapstick clown isn't really suffering. And we know that Arnolphe really is. But we either shrug off or laugh off his suffering because his obsession makes him potentially evil, and we know that he must be made to suffer in order to prevent him from inflicting suffering on others. Molière himself *played* Arnolphe's "desperate, moving words" for laughs, but one eminent critic has suggested that Molière may not have *written* them for laughs—a perceptive statement indicating awareness of Molière's ability to realize that the pangs of jealous and unrequited love can be genuine and at the same time ridiculous. Like the dying poet-clown in *La Strada*, he had the courage to jest at his own suffering, especially if it resulted from what his relentless judgment obliged him to admit was folly. Even in his last moments, while he was playing the *Imaginary Invalid*, he tried by forcing a laugh to hide the convulsion that killed him.

Throughout the centuries Arnolphe has been played as a comedy character, but from time to time actors have introduced both tragic and farcical elements which it is safe to say are foreign to Molière's conception of Arnolphe. He has been played as a dirty old man pressuring a maiden pure as the driven snow into marriage. As Molière saw him and played him, he was neither dirty nor old. The difference in age between him and his ward was considerable, but not monstrous. Nor is Arnolphe as he was played by Provost at the turn of the century—a quasi-Byronic type, elegant, enlightened, generous, marred by a single tragic flaw, his obsession with Agnes. Nor yet is he the Arnolphe of Lucien Guitry, who in the early 1920's uttered passionate sex cries which prevented him from being in the least amusing. Possibly the most authentic Arnolphe of all was created by Louis Jouvet, to whom we owe the vogue *School For Wives* has enjoyed since 1936. Like Provost's, Jouvet's Arnolphe is youngish and elegant, but there the resemblance ends. He is a predominantly ludicrous character right from the start. He is both over-confident and anxious. He is positive that the cuckoldry which he believes befalls most husbands will not befall him—and at the same time mortally afraid that it will. His agony is undeniable, but even when he falls abjectly on his knees and implores Agnes not to leave him, Jouvet speedily erases the effect of this painful scene by involving him in a game of hide-and-seek with Horace a few moments after. When he meets his doom he suffers, as do all the arrogant when stripped of their pretentions. But his discomfiture is not in the least tragic. He has committed no crime (though he sought mightily to violate the natural law) and so he is neither fined nor banished nor doomed to die either by his own hand or that of a foe. His sole offence is folly, and he is treated as all fools should—simply laughed off the stage.

Like Arnolphe, Agnes, the most intriguing of Molière's heroines, has been variously interpreted and misinterpreted throughout the years. Molière is partly to blame for there being some doubt as to the scope of her attainments. Arnolphe, no doubt indulging in slight hyperbole, tells us "she would have difficulty spelling *cat*," and she is supposed to be so ignorant that her reading of the Maxims of Marriage is a slow process. Yet her letter to Horace is charming both in sentiment and in style, and it is presumably properly spelled and punctuated into the bargain! But Molière has left little excuse for misinterpretation of her character. Nothing in the script seems to justify her being played as a sophisticated miss slily outwitting a doddering old man—or as a sort of pre-Nabokov Lolita—and yet she has been so played. At the other extreme she has been made so over-ingenuous as to be insipid. Molière's clear intention was to stress how she evolved in the course of the play. At the outset she is both ignorant and stupid, as all intelligent people are stupid who have never had a chance to develop their intelligence. But in two days' time both Arnolphe and Horace feed her a series of cram courses which make her bud and blossom (as flowers do in a few seconds in the movies) into a full-blown rose—or tiger lily. As far as we know, this transformation is what her first interpreter, Mademoiselle De Brie, sought successfully to convey. Madeleine Ozeray, who played Agnes to Jouvet's Arnolphe, made her evolution intensely dramatic. She indeed strengthened the role of Agnes to such an extent that, although Agnes has only 190 lines to Arnolphe's 840, the play became what it had never been before—a duet instead of a solo. In addition Madeleine Ozeray supplied the semi-tragic overtones which Jouvet was careful to avoid in his portrayal of Arnolphe. What her audiences witnessed was certainly what Molière had in mind: "not only the awakening of love, but the emergence of a personality." While she showed Agnes evolving from the helpless child of the first act to the near-vixen of the fifth, as she defies the maniac who proposes to rob her of what she knows to be her happiness, it was easy to understand why it has been said that in the whole theatre of Molière no heroine can compare with Agnes.

School For Wives consolidated the reputation Molière had won with *The Precious Ladies* and *School For Husbands*. It naturally exacerbated the fury of his literary rivals who, "speechless with rage," attacked him in pamphlets and epistles with a vehemence that is without parallel in literary history. Molière demolished their niggling criticisms in his *Critique of The School For Wives* and his *Versailles Impromptu*, leaving them impotent of all but accusing him, falsely, of incest and jeering at his wife's infidelities.

An equally implacable and much more dangerous foe was the band of religious bigots who pounced on the famous *double entendre* in Act 2 to brand the play immoral, and on the ten Maxims of Marriage to "prove" Molière guilty of sacrilegiously satirizing the Ten Commandments. Curiously, the passage that contains the most dynamite seems to have roused the least furore, namely, the debate on sex and marriage in Act 3. Arnolphe has just informed his ward that sexual indulgence is frowned upon by God except when practiced within the bonds of holy matrimony. Which prompts the following questions from Agnes:

> If you're not married, it's a sin—you're sure?
> Married, those sinful kisses are all pure?

ARNOLPHE: Precisely.

AGNES: Unwed, love's a foul disease?
But once you're wed, you can do all you please?

ARNOLPHE: Of course.

This, Agnes indicates, makes scant sense to her. This passage, incidentally, may have inspired Shaw's discussion in *Man and Superman* of the same subject, which concludes with his famous aphorism: "Virtue is the Trades Unionism of the married." At all events, it cannot have endeared Molière with the rigidly righteous of his day, whom he was brave enough and foolish enough to attack in *Tartuffe*, and who retaliated by denying him decent burial and by pursuing him even beyond the grave. Time has pronounced *School For Wives* a wholesome, not an immoral, play, and has vindicated Molière as it eventually does all men of good will. Even in clerical circles today it is generally, if reluctantly, conceded that Molière and Agnes were on the side of the angels, while Arnolphe and the bigots were indeed "of the devil."

INTRODUCTION

PART THREE

The Translation

To translate a play is to tamper with it. This is true even if you are translating a play into prose. It is even more true if you are translating it into blank verse. It is inevitable if you are translating it into rhymed verse. The exigencies of rhyme and rhythm must, of course, never force you into distorting any of the playwright's ideas. These twin tyrants must never drive you to perversion. But they may occasionally oblige you to resort to inversion, though you often will be able to compensate by avoiding inversion where the playwright, as vulnerable a victim as you to the demands of rhyme and rhythm, has been unable to do so.

Since tampering with a text is generally frowned upon, why translate a text into rhymed verse, when putting it into prose would not only produce a more "accurate" version, but would make the task infinitely less laborious? The obvious answer is that if the author has seen fit to use rhyme, there is no alternative to translating his work into rhyme. Imagine Pope's "Rape of the Lock" rendered into French prose! In short, since there is no such thing as an "accurate" translation of any text worthy of being described as a work of art, the sole concern of the translator must be to remain scrupulously faithful, not to the letter of the text, but to the spirit and the flavor of it.

To "tamper" with the literal text is indeed often the only way of remaining faithful to its spirit. In fact, if one pays more than mere lip service to Molière's dictum that the greatest rule of all is to give pleasure, one finds oneself obliged to take considerable liberties with the literal text. If, for example, an allusion which was undoubtedly relished by the author's contemporaries is meaningless today, the translator is surely under the obligation to substitute an allusion which will be relished by *his* contemporaries. The alternative would be to explain the allusion in a scholarly footnote which would take all the starch out of it for the reader, if he took the trouble to read it, and would, of course, keep the allusion meaningless for the audience. However accurate the "translation" of such an allusion might be, it would in a comedy fail to be funny and so militate against the spirit of the original. Acting out of this conviction, I have converted one of these obscure allusions intended to indicate the depths of Agnes's ignorance thus: "She cannot tell cream cheese from chromosome," achieving an alliteration and at the same perpetrating—but without the slightest sense of guilt—an anachronism of the sort for which William Shakespeare was always being hauled over the coals!

The idiom of any fairly remote period also demands very free translation. In all his plays Molière makes liberal use of colloquialisms, many of which have ceased to be current in twentieth-century French. Whereas some of these may be rendered by 17th or 18th century English colloquialisms which are still generally understood today,

such as the expletives, "Zounds" and "Egad, "others may
not. Consequently they have to be rendered by colloquialisms meaningful to contemporary audiences and
readers. That is precisely why new translations of masterpieces which are "not of an age but for all time" have to
be made every generation.

This translator's first glimpse of these truths came some
years ago when he was asked by the college theatre
director to adapt the hilarious epilogue to Molière's
Imaginary Invalid for a forthcoming production of the play.
Both play and epilogue were well received by the mainly
student audience, whose enjoyment of the latter was not
diminished by the fact that the cast consisted of usually
staid and venerable professors. Then came *Tartuffe*, which
attracted considerable lay as well as college audiences and
abundantly proved that there are no grounds for the
uneasy belief that, verse drama being relatively rare today,
amateur actors might find verse too hard to handle.[1] The
obvious answer to this anxiety is that both rhyme and
rhythm should be allowed to take care of themselves—
which they are perfectly capable of doing. The ease and
naturalness wherewith the cast disposed of the script con-
clusively indicated that this is so. *Tartuffe* was followed by
Cyrano de Bergerac, and if any play demands the piquancy
which Pope and Dryden had equipped the heroic couplet
to deliver, it is surely the masterpiece of Rostand. Several
prose and blank verse translations have adequately rendered the meaning of the lines, but—to paraphrase Mark

[1] *It is interesting to note how fashions change. When Molière staged THE
MISER, his audiences were somewhat shocked by his offering them a five-act play
in prose. And an enemy of his who grudgingly admitted there was merit in his
early one-act comedy, THE PRECIOUS LADIES, proceeded to "improve"
it by rendering it into verse!*

Twain, they have dismally failed to give us the tune. Admittedly an English version in babytalk for second graders would be far from dull. But *Cyrano de Bergerac* cries out for the constant clamor of the rhyme, tamper though it may and must with Rostand's text.

In further defence of tampering, it may be stated that Louis Jouvet, possibly the most brilliant interpreter of Molière of all time, did not hesitate to tamper with the script of *School For Wives* more than any mere translator would presume to do. Not only did he rearrange Act III, but he showed how well he understood Molière's cheerful indifference to the implausibility of the ending by tacking on to it a brief ballet of the sort to which Molière was so partial, and which Molière might well have added himself if he had had time to think of it. Compared with this, my own tampering is, I trust, venial. My only deviation from the text is in Act 2, where I decided to make a dialogue out of Agnes' interminable reading of the famous Maxims of Marriage. I felt somewhat tempted to break up some of the other lengthy monologues as well, but resisted because they are mainly narrative in character and so, as Molière claimed, are actually the equivalent of action. Agnes's lengthy, uninterrupted, and painfully slow recital obviously is not. It was an ordeal for her, but I see no reason why it should be an ordeal for the audience. I am well aware that Agnes's distaste for this required reading has been interpreted as further excuse for her revolt and final emancipation. Molière may indeed have so intended it. But if he did, Arnold's constant and complacent approval of the loathed maxims could only intensify her loathing. Besides, the verbal fencing between the pair brings out what might be called the ingenious ingenuousness of Agnes and the asininity of her guardian. Finally their bickering interchange adds a further touch of humor to the play, and if the nature of some of it may be thought to be less characteristic of Molière than of Bob Hope, Jack Benny, Ogden Nash or Tom Lehrer, it can only be retorted that a) it would be hard to prove that it is uncharacteristic of Molière and b) Molière would have been the last to disparage these fun- and satire-dispensers of our times.

As for the style of my translation, I have endeavored in this as in everything else, to parallel Molière's, which as the critics have agreed, is in his high comedy a mixture of the dignified language characteristic of tragedy and of the vernacular, which is common to farce. In my use of inversion I have been, I believe, neither more nor less liberal than Molière. Here and there he was forced into using an awkward inversion.[1] So occasionally have I been. Take, for example, the couplet:

> If by your work you were so occupied,
> How did it happen that this wretch you spied?

The inversion in the second line is clearly dictated by the necessity of getting a rhyme for "occupied," and, though the meaning is clear, the order is not the normal order of prose. The inversion of the first line is, however, acceptable in prose, as is true of a number of other conscious and purposeful inversions. Take for example,

> The woman's virtue I'd heard often praised.

---

[1] *The author of a book on Louis Jouvet, whose Arnolphe was unforgetable, commends Jouvet's rendering of the text "despite some difficult versification."*

Instead of this I could as easily have written:

I'd often heard the woman's virtue praised.

I preferred the first version, however, as a means of lending variety and emphasis by deviating from the tedious subject-verb sentence or clause opening.

When I embarked on this translation, I knew of no English version of *School*, never having had any occasion to use one. While I was in the middle of it, my attention was drawn to the fact that Professor Morris Bishop had produced one. I purposely avoided reading it until long after my own was complete. I have since read it, and have found to my relief that it is mainly in blank verse, with no rhyme whatsoever except in the Maxims. Whereas it is as competent as everything else that Professor Bishop has produced, I consider the lack of rhyme, for above-mentioned reasons, a matter for regret. The only other "translation" I have since discovered is an adaptation in three acts by Miles Mallison. This, though masquerading as verse, is actually prose and therefore holds up a dull mirror to Molière.

My own aim is simple, however hard it may be to achieve, and however imperfectly I may have achieved it —to make my translation identical, not literally, but in the fullest sense of the word, with the original—that is, to make *School For Wives* as meaningful and amusing for 20th century audiences as *L'Ecole des Femmes* was for the audiences of Molière's day.

CHARACTERS

ARNOLPHE,   a Paris bourgeois also known as Monsieur de la Souche.

AGNES,   a charming but uneducated girl—Arnolphe's ward.

HORACE,   a dashing young man in love with Agnes.

ALLAN,   a stupid peasant employed by Arnolphe as a servant.

GEORGETTE,   likewise.

CHRYSALDE,   a friend of Arnolphe's.

ENRIQUE,   Chrysalde's brother-in-law.

ORONTE,   Horace's father and a very old friend of Arnolphe's.

The action takes place in a public square in Paris. The gate leading to Arnolphe's house is prominent. A garden downstage right makes a fairly plausible setting for some of the more intimate scenes.

ACT ONE

CHRYSALDE: Your business here, then, is to ask her hand?

ARNOLPHE: (*firmly*) Tomorrow! ...That is what I've planned.

CHRYSALDE: (*solicitous*) Here we can talk in private—
without fear
Lest what we say will fall on prying ear...
I'll tell you frankly, then, what's in my heart:
I'm troubled by the news that you impart!
Whether this marriage is post-haste or tardy,
For you the enterprise is most foolhardy!

ARNOLPHE: (*taking umbrage at once*) Perhaps *your*
marriage has had slight success—
So *mine*, forsooth, must spell unhappiness
For me! The same shoe fits both me and you.
Your wife is frivolous—*Mine* will be too!

CHRYSALDE: My friend, it happens to the best of men.
Without reflection I could name you ten.
They've been unfortunate—but they're not to blame.
And no one's sought to cover them with shame
But you! That's why I fear what will befall
You, if in turn *you* meet the fate they've all

I

Encountered. When they heard you jibe and jeer,
They winced. When *your* wife cheats on *you*, they'll
  cheer!
They've all seen how you relish every scandal—
And sometimes you've had more than you could handle!

ARNOLPHE: Indeed I have—and I'm ashamed to think
No other city you can name's a sink
Of sin like Paris! Travel far and wide—
You'll find no husbands so devoid of pride!
One makes a fortune—which his wife expends
On lovers, hell-bent for ignoble ends.
Another—furious—makes a great commotion....
Of taking action, though, he hasn't a notion!
Another spies the lover at his gate,
And finds some pretext to evaporate.
Grabbing his shoes up from the closet floor,
The lover sneaks out through the servants' door!...
The wives, of course, are even a shade more vile!

  (*He catches Chrysalde's look of amusement*)

I fail to understand how you can smile!...
One meets her lover every day in bed,
And tells her husband he's been long since dead!
One says from gaming all her money came—
Only she doesn't specify which game!
Whereat the husband thanks God for her luck!
What can I do but jeer! For that's the ruck
Of married folk in Paris, you'll admit.

CHRYSALDE: Maybe—but by what right do you, sir, sit
In judgment? I don't approve of all I see,
But if the self-same fate were to o'ertake me,
I think I would win sympathy—not scorn ...
Not you, though! .... Far too often have you torn
Your friends asunder with your fangs! Beware!
They'll slaughter *you* if *you're* caught in that snare!

ARNOLPHE: Have no anxiety on my behalf,
My friend... I know these females, and I laugh
At them. I know the tricks the jades employ
To plunge their mates in pain while they enjoy
The fruits of their deception—every one!
Forewarned's forearmed—I will not be undone! ...
I just won't pick a smart one for a mate...
You see, it's simpler far than eight times eight!

CHRYSALDE: In your opinion, then, no man is right
Who'd wed a woman that is half-way bright?

ARNOLPHE: Precisely! ... Wed a fool—or else *BE* one!

CHRYSALDE: My wife's no fool, and yet she hasn't
begun—

ARNOLPHE:
To cheat you yet!... That's all, my friend—just wait!
You too will soon be moaning of your fate ...
Paris is full of husbands who repent
Of wedding wives who were intelligent!
Women men take for better or for worse
Had better not be smart—else they're a curse!

I've seen too many of my friends in pain
Because they married in their haste—a brain!

CHRYSALDE: If grain of folly doesn't make man an ass,
How can a pinch of wit destroy a lass?

ARNOLPHE: I'll tell you how! ... She'll spend the livelong
   day
In talk—of poetry, art, the latest play,
Which she'll attend, decked in the latest style
(A sight to make all decent women smile) ...
She even may get herself a fifth-rate part.
The author then proceeds to steal her—heart,
Wondering just who the dunderpate can be
Who lets her out on this perpetual spree!

CHRYSALDE: You have no partiality for wits, I see!

ARNOLPHE: Egad, a clever woman gives me fits!
The worst are those who fancy they can write,
They sit up making verses half the night—
Or so they say—when you unlock the door
To let *her* Highness in at half past four!

CHRYSALDE: Come now, my friend, you *do* exaggerate!
My clever wife does not come home so late.

ARNOLPHE: Some fop or dandy's always at their side ...
The sight of these I simply can't abide.
I'd never dream of marrying one such!
One who can read and write knows *far too much*,
Say I! ... To be the carriage's fifth wheel
May be *your* dream! Bravo for you! I feel

I'd rather be the driver! Keep her *home!*
Though she can't tell cream cheese from chromosome,
If she can cook and mend and go to mass,
Then in my school for wives she'll surely pass!

CHRYSALDE: In short—a stupid wife is what *you* seek.

ARNOLPHE: I do! I would not take a second peek
Even at a raving beauty if I thought
She was a trifle smarter than she ought!
I do not care how dumb mine acts and looks
If she but goes to mass and sews and cooks!

CHRYSALDE: Yes, you said some such thing before.

ARNOLPHE: Let's have no further doubt, then, on that score!
Virtue's enough for me.

CHRYSALDE: But can a fool
Be virtuous? ... She may know the golden rule,
And so do more for others than she should!
Much more, in fact, than would be for her good! ...
And must a woman of intelligence
Inevitably yearn to leap the fence,
Even though she's married to a worthy man?

ARNOLPHE: Talk all day if you like! ... I'm sure you can!

CHRYSALDE: I'll say no more. It's your affair, I know.

ARNOLPHE: The wife I wed I will not wed for show!

CHRYSALDE: Oh, don't apologize—each to his taste!

ARNOLPHE: The maid whom at this moment I'm in haste

To wed is—frankly—all I could demand.
She's meek, she's modest—and I'm sure her hand
'S mine for the asking... She is very poor.
I've planned to marry her since she was four!

CHRYSALDE: She's—eligibly dumb?

ARNOLPHE: I've seen to that!
She would have difficulty spelling "cat."

CHRYSALDE: And she's responded to your flame, of course?

ARNOLPHE: You didn't think I'd taken her by force!
She is an orphan—by a peasant raised—
The woman's virtue I'd heard often praised—
Her abject poverty caused me distress;
I felt I might relieve its bitter stress,
And so I took the child beneath my wing.
You see, it seemed the charitable thing
To do ...

CHRYSALDE: Of course!

ARNOLPHE: At the same time I knew
I'd have a wife who'd not be taken aback
At what perhaps in rank and wealth I lack.

CHRYSALDE: I follow.

ARNOLPHE: She was happy to accept.
"As nature made her, so I want her kept!"
I said ... A convent thus I chose, remote
From cities' hum, where she would learn by rote
All that was fitting for a wife to know—

And nothing more! I emphasized they should
Preserve her just as stupid as they could!
Thank God, my fondest dreams met with success.
Nothing you've known can match the emptiness
Of her young mind! ... Thus she's been raised
That gratefully I murmur, "Heaven be praised!"
She is the wife for me—to order made!

CHRYSALDE: Of such a wife I'd be a mite afraid ...

ARNOLPHE: I took her from the convent—looked around
For some abode ... In my own house are found
Some whom I'd just as soon not have her meet ...
Right from the start, you see, I've been discreet.

CHRYSALDE: I always knew you were a reprobate!
Once you are wed, you will be more sedate,
I trust!

ARNOLPHE: Of course ... Don't interrupt me, please! ...
I put her in a lodging where she sees—
Well—not a soul who's not as dumb as she—
Except, of course, occasionally—me.

CHRYSALDE: How cosy! ... So you feel you've kept her
pure?

ARNOLPHE: If I am sure of aught, of that I'm sure!
See for yourself! Dine with us both tonight!

CHRYSALDE: If my smart wife agrees, I guess I might.

ARNOLPHE: And if you find she's brighter than I said,
I give you leave to—why—chop off my head!

CHRYSALDE: I'm still convinced that you exaggerate.

ARNOLPHE: I swear her guilelessness I *under*rate,
Chrysalde! ... A hundred things the little witch's
Enquired would put a Chinaman in stitches!
Just yesterday she was all exercised
Over a point you'd never have surmised:
"Do babies come from cabbage or by stork?!"

CHRYSALDE: Danger for you, I fear, Arnolphe, may lurk
In such unnatural innocence ... Beware!
Such virgins become mothers unaware!

ARNOLPHE: (*stung*) Thanks! ... And I'd thank you still
   more to recall
That I don't like the name Arnolphe at all!
Arnolphe's the patron saint of you know whom—
Husbands whose folly's led them to a doom
I will avoid! ... *They* may need help from heaven,
But not to *me* will their saint's name be given!

CHRYSALDE: A thousand pardons, Monsieur de la
   Souche! ...
My view (I will not beat about the bush)
Is that at forty-two it's rather strange
To take a rotten tree-stump on your range
And coin yourself a fancy name from it!
To me that's no sign of outstanding wit!

ARNOLPHE: La Souche's the name I've given my estate—
My name should be the same, I estimate!

CHRYSALDE: (*malicious*) A peasant called Big Joe, I
    understand,
  Dug a ditch round his wretched plot of land,
  Filled it with muddy water—and he styles
  Himself today, forsooth—Lord of the Isles!

ARNOLPHE: Your tale is in poor taste, sir! Make an end,
  If you'd have De la Souche remain your friend!

CHRYSALDE: For others you are still "Arnolphe," I see.
  But—you'll be Monsieur de la Souche for me.

ARNOLPHE: Thank you ... Farewell! ... I'm stopping here
    to say
  I'm back again, and bid her a good day.

(*As he moves towards the gate of the house in which he has
    lodged Agnes, he says*)

He thinks himself a Socrates, that's plain.
But any fool can see the man's insane!

CHRYSALDE: (*on his way out*) Strange how a man gets so
    convinced he's right!
  He strides around just asking for a fight!
                        (*Exit Chrysalde*)

ARNOLPHE: (*approaching the gate*) Ho, there!

ALLAN: (*on the other side*) Who's there?

ARNOLPHE: Why, open up! It's me! ...
  I never dreamed ten days so long could be!

ALLAN: Who is it?

ARNOLPHE: Me, I said!

ALLAN: Georgette!

GEORGETTE: (*also on the other side*)   Well what?

ARNOLPHE: (*to himself*)   These two are even stupider than I thought!

ALLAN: (*to Georgette*)   Open the door!

GEORGETTE: (*to Allan*)   *You* go!

ALLAN: *You* go!

GEORGETTE: I won't!

ALLAN: Neither will I!

ARNOLPHE: (*frothing*)   I'll brain you if you don't This very minute! ... Open up, I say!

ALLAN: Who's there?

ARNOLPHE: *Your master!*

GEORGETTE:

ALLAN: What?

GEORGETTE: It's him! Allan!
                         Open up fast!

ALLAN: *You* open!

ARNOLPHE: Shake a limb,
                         I tell you!!

GEORGETTE: No, I've got to shake the mat!

ALLAN: I've got to save the sparrow from the cat! ... *woops!*

ARNOLPHE: (*trying to make the fools understand*)
   Now one of you two won't unbar this door!

That one won't eat for three days—or for four.

(*They both rush to open*)

GEORGETTE: Don't bother, Allan—I'm already there!

ALLAN: Too late, Georgette—your efforts we can spare!

GEORGETTE: *I*'ll open!

ALLAN: *I* will!

GEORGETTE: You won't!

ALLAN: Nor will you!

ARNOLPHE: Patience like mine's vouchsafed to precious few!

ALLAN: *I* opened, sir!

GEORGETTE: *I* did!

ALLAN: I'd box your ear,
You lying jade, if Monsieur were not here!

(*They overwhelm Arnolphe with solicitude*)

ARNOLPHE: Look out, you oaf! ...

ALLAN: Oh, pardon!

ARNOLPHE: What a clown!
Between the two of you, you'll have me down! ...
Come, pull yourselves together! Give me news!

BOTH: We've both been well!

ARNOLPHE: How long will you abuse
My patience, sirrah! Zounds! *Keep* your hat off!

(*This is the third time Arnolphe has removed Allan's hat!*)

ALLAN: I'm sorry, sir!

You *will* be! ... Now, be off!
Go fetch my bride-to-be! ... You, Georgette, stay!...
Was your young mistress sad with me away?

GEORGETTE: Why no! Why should she?

ARNOLPHE: (*menacing*)   Not sad? ... No?

GEORGETTE: (*catching on*)   Oh yes!
The picture of a damsel in distress! ...
When in the street she heard a donkey pass,
She'd clap her hands and cry, "He's back!"—poor lass!

(*As Agnes approaches, Arnolphe eyes her approvingly.*)

ARNOLPHE: She brings her sewing. Good! ... Agnes, good
   day!
I have come back, you see—come back to stay,
Perhaps, my dear. Now, would that make you glad?

AGNES: Oh yes it would ... You know I'm seldom sad.

ARNOLPHE: I'm glad to see you, Agnes, and to hear
That in my absence you've been happy here.

AGNES: Oh yes, sir, thank you—save for all the fleas.
I've never seen fleas half so big as these!

ARNOLPHE: Well, Agnes, if you wish, I think I might
See you're protected from them every night.

AGNES: That would be nice.

ARNOLPHE: It shall be as you ask.
Giving you pleasure's a delightful task ...
I see you have been busy ... What is that?

AGNES: Oh that, I think 's, a pretty lady's hat ...
(*But the light in her eyes dies as she continues!*)
I've done the nightcaps and the gowns for you.

ARNOLPHE: A busy woman is a gay one too ...
But now I'm sure you've earned a little rest.
Return, dear Agnes, to your cosy nest ...
When I come back, we'll sit down to discuss
Some business that concerns only us.

(*Exit Agnes—Arnolphe turns to the audience.*)

Now all you ladies who think you're so smart—
Who love to talk philosophy and art—
With your refinement and your so-called grace—
The costly ointments you smear on your face—
All your grand airs, your elegance, your wit—
If you would on yourselves in judgment sit,
Would you presume to match your decadence
With her unspoiled, unsullied innocence! ...
Virtue's the thing! ...

(*He catches sight of someone who turns out to be Horace*)

But who's this? ... Can it be?
No no, it can't! ... Yes, bless my heart, it's he!
Why, Horace!

HORACE: Arnolphe!

ARNOLPHE: Horace! I'm delighted!
When was it that in Paris you alighted?

HORACE: Nine days ago ... Came here without delay,
And learned with grief that you'd just gone away!

ARNOLPHE: Yes, I spent ten long days on my estate.
And I'm right glad I've not returned too late
To show you our fair city ... My, you've grown!
Ah, you remind me how the years have flown!
Last time I saw you you were but so high.

HORACE: Soon, like Jack's beanstalk, I will hit the sky!

ARNOLPHE: How's my good friend your father—dear
Oronte?
I've known him right from the baptismal font!
But it must be eight long years since last we met ...
He used to cut a caper! ... Does he yet?

HORACE: His friends insist he's livelier far than I.
He sends you this.

(*He gives Arnolphe a letter*)

But since—I know not why—
He writes to say he will himself be here.
One of his cronies who spent many a year
In Ecuador or Paraguay—'tis told—
Is back home with gigantic piles of gold!

ARNOLPHE: Who can it be?

HORACE: It seems Enrique's the name.

ARNOLPHE: I vaguely know the man—but not his fame.

HORACE: Howbeit, he and father have th'intention
To execute some business they don't mention.

ARNOLPHE: Your tidings are as welcome as choice wine.
Friends of your father are as surely mine!

(*He reads the letter*)

A charming letter—which he might have spared
Himself the pain of writing. I'm prepared—
And always will be—till my days are done,
To cater to the wants of Oronte's son.

HORACE: I'm glad to find in you a friend indeed,
For surely you'll find me a friend in need! ...
I need a hundred crowns, to be exact!

ARNOLPHE: Now that I know your needs, sir, I can act.

(*He gives him his purse*)

Here's more than you require—and—keep the purse.
They both are yours for better or for worse!

HORACE: Your kindness leaves me speechless!

ARNOLPHE: Then don't speak ...
The pleasure's mine ... So you've been here a week?
You've walked our streets. Paris has been your host.
I'd like to know what has impressed you most.

HORACE: The crowds! The buildings! These Elysian
                                        Fields!
What joy their throng of pretty women yields!

ARNOLPHE: Each has his own idea of the good life ...
Surely for him who loves his neighbor's wife
Paris is paradise! The wives are—kind,
And nine tenths of the husbands just don't mind.

Pick the exact type you would like to get—
A tall, a short, a blonde, or a brunette ...
I'm quite content to be a mere spectator.
But *you're* cut out for a participator!
A handsome youth like you is all they ask.
And duping a dull husband is no task ...
In fact, if none have cast on you sheep's eyes
Already, I'll learn so with great surprise!

HORACE: I will speak frankly ... Yes, there *is* one here
Whom I've already come to hold most dear ...
While prudence counsels me th'affair to hide,
I'm somehow forced by friendship to confide
To you th'events whose ending makes me wretch
Or conqueror.

ARNOLPHE: One moment—let me fetch
My journal. I foresee the sort of tale
Wherewith in my old age I shall regale
Myself.

HORACE: Please keep it *to* yourself—and me—
Or else you'll plunge me deep in misery ...
To get, in love's sweet game, from word to deed,
Discretion is the virtue that we need.

ARNOLPHE: Come, count on me!

HORACE: I do ... The girl I love—
She's young, she's fair, she's gentle as a dove!

ARNOLPHE: They're all like that!

HORACE: She smiles on my advances! ...
   In fact, I'd wager fifty crowns my chance is
   Good of calling her by week's end—mine!

ARNOLPHE: Bravo! ... I wonder who'll be next in line!

HORACE: My heart is hers—and hers it will remain,
   I swear!

ARNOLPHE: You're young. Were I you, I'd refrain
   From swearing! But just where does she reside—
   This damsel you'd have always at your side?

HORACE: This you won't credit! Why, she lives close by!
   From here you should be able to descry
   The house ... Of course you can! ... It's—

ARNOLPHE: *Not* the one
   Across the street??

HORACE: It is!

ARNOLPHE: (*aside*)   Ah, I'm undone!

HORACE: Looks like a prison—yes ... It's there my pearl
   Is closely guarded by a jealous churl.
   They say he hopes to keep her free from harm
   By making her a dunce ... Ah, but the charm
   With which this creature is endowed
   Is such that lack of schooling cannot cloud
   Its brilliance! So enchanting is her air
   Men will fall down before her everywhere!
   Her smile would melt a Tartar or a Moor!
   In wealth alone is this rare damsel poor ...
   Perhaps you have seen her. Agnes is her name!

ARNOLPHE: !!!!!

HORACE: The loathsome wretch who plays this nasty game
With her is called la Zouche or Couche, they say.
From all accounts he gets more mad each day ...
But you must know him since he lives so near.

ARNOLPHE: !!!!!

HORACE: I'm sorry, but I fear I failed to hear ...
Do you or don't you?

ARNOLPHE: I ... suppose I ... do.

HORACE: Then you'd agree he's mad too, wouldn't you?

ARNOLPHE: !!!!!

HORACE: All Paris knows he's just a jealous fool
Who thought to keep poor Agnes out of school
And so enslave her ... Thirteen years he's toiled
For that! *My* business is to see he's foiled! ...
This means two persons must be bought and sold...
Ah, there's no substitute, Arnolphe, for gold
In love and war! ... And that's where *you* come in.
Without *your* crowns I'd stand no chance to win
My love .... But you look grieved! It surely can
Not be that you should disapprove my plan?

ARNOLPHE: No ... I was thinking ...

HORACE: Of something else? I see ...
What an infernal bore you must find me! ...
Thank you for listening just the same, dear friend.
Together we'll win through to happy end!   (*Exit*)

ARNOLPHE: This is too much ....

> (*Horace rushes back*)
> I just came back to say
A careless word could give me clean away!
Please be discreet!   (*Exit again*)

ARNOLPHE: Yes, yes!

> (*Horace is back again*)

HORACE: Don't tell my dad!
You never know. Somehow he might get mad!

> (*Exit finally*)

ARNOLPHE: I wonder whether, since the world began,
Such anguish has been felt by mortal man!
I will go mad if I don't use my wit
To put—once and for all—an end to it ...
But how?... I was a fool to let him go!
He would have babbled on—and now I'd know
What—if it's true—will strike me to the ground—
That Agnes, lost to me, in him has found
A lover! ... If I run, I'll catch him yet!
Ply him with cunning questions till I get
The truth from him, and learn the worst—or best.
Until I do, I'll know nor peace nor rest!

> (*Exit running. Blackout*)

ACT TWO

ARNOLPHE: (*Alone—and realizing Horace has outdistanced him*)

I've lost him! ... Well, perhaps it's better thus.
My pain would have been far too obvious.
And at this stage I cannot have him know
It was at *me* he dealt this cruel blow ...
I will not let this whippersnapper rule,
Though! I will not submit to be his fool!
One point, then, I need information on:
Just how far have the cursed couple gone?
My husband's honor is at stake, 'od's life!
Already I consider her my wife.
Is she has fallen, more than half the shame
Will be attached by gossip to *my* name ...
What prompted me to stay away so long!
It was not only foolish—it was wrong!

(*He knocks at the door and Allan answers immediately*)

ALLAN: I'm opening *this* time, sir, you see! ...

ARNOLPHE: Come here,

You stupid pair! I want you both to hear!
You understand?

(*The stupid pair know what's coming*)

20

GEORGETTE: Oh mercy, master, please!
See—we both ask for it on bended knees!

ARNOLPHE: You waste your time! Give me one reason
                                                    why
Both you vile traitors don't deserve to die!

ALLAN: He's not himself today—that's clear to me.

GEORGETTE: Those nasty things just can't be meant for
                                                    we!

ARNOLPHE: Silence! ... Why, I'm so angry I can't speak!
Imagine! I've been scarcely gone a week—
And you ...! Who was it told you to permit
A man to enter? ... Who told you to admit
Anyone! ... Who?

                         (*They are in a mood to run away*)

                         Stay, you idiots, stay!
I'll massacre the first who runs away! ...
Now, tell me—How did he get in—this foe
Of mine? ... Now, quick! No nonsense! I must know!

BOTH: Oh, mercy, master!

GEORGETTE: I feel faint!

ALLAN: I swoon!

ARNOLPHE: *You* swoon? ... Death will be *mine* this after-
    noon!
I'm drunk with rage and fear—a deadly brew!
And whom to thank for this foul draught but *you!* ...
Who would have dreamed this harmless, chubby boy

Would have grown up to plague me and employ
His—youth against me! ... What the wretch has done
My only hope of finding out's from one—
Agnes! ... Go fetch her! ... No, you'd better not.
You'd tell her how upset I am, you sot!
And she'd be on her guard ... Be still, my heart!
I must be calm to play this cunning part.
I'll go myself to fetch her. You stay here!

(*Exit Arnolphe*)

GEORGETTE: I've never known master act so queer!
If looks could kill, we'd be as dead as toads.

ALLAN: I think he's angry ... Mark my words! This bodes
No good for me and you and Agnes' beau!

GEORGETTE: *There's* something now I'd give a lot to
    know:
Why shut her up in jail day after day?
Night too? Just why keep other men away
From her?

ALLAN: Because he's jealous. That is all!

GEORGETTE: Now I don't get this jealousy at all.
What makes him jealous? Why does he get mad
At this young man? He's quite a pleasant lad.

ALLAN: All right, I'll tell you ... Well, you see, Georgette,
When you get jealous—why—you're all upset.
No cure for jealousy has yet been found...
You're scared of every man who hangs around ...

(pause while Georgette ponders this)

If the idea's too hard for you to seize,
Here's an example you will grasp with ease:
Suppose you've got a bowl of soup between your knees,
And someone, without even an "if you please,"
Dips her fat fingers in it—wouldn't you
Be tempted to raise quite a hullaballoo?

GEORGETTE: Fat fingers in my soup? ... Would I get mad?
I surely would, whether't be lass or lad!

ALLAN: Well, jealousy's like that! That's what!
Woman is man's soup. So, you see, he's not
The least bit pleased when someone comes along
And helps himself ... And who can say he's wrong?

GEORGETTE: I understand ... But then I think it's strange
That all men don't get mad when others range
In their preserves. Some husbands aren't proud
Unless their wife's surrounded by a crowd
Of panting lovers, waiting for their turn!

ALLAN: Georgette, I see you've still got lots to learn!
Some men aren't greedy—therefore they don't worry.
Our master, though, 's not in *that* category!

(Arnolphe appears)

GEORGETTE: Unless my eyes deceive—

ALLAN: They don't. It's him.

GEORGETTE: I wish it weren't! ... My, but he looks grim!

ARNOLPHE: *(doing his best to keep cool)*

A Greek once said to Emperor Augustus
And not, I think, without a certain justice—
Action in anger's good—but better yet
Is—stop and repeat the entire alphabet.
This gives a man the time to simmer down
And so avoid being laughed at all through town...
I'll soon find out how useful this advice is
In helping me cope with the current crisis.
I'll be completely calm ...
   (*but he can't quite!*)

                A, B, C, D ...

It seems to work. (*He bursts out again*)
The villain! ..... E, F, G .....

           (*He gains temporary control of himself*)

Agnes, I'm waiting ... Come, join me, my sweet! ...
You two—get back in off the street!

       (*Enter Agnes and they set out on their walk*)

This is a lovely walk, my dear!

AGNES: It is.

ARNOLPHE: The weather's lovely too, my dear!

AGNES: It is.

ARNOLPHE: Tell me ... What's happened here since my
   last visit?

  The question's quite discreet, I trust ... Or is it?

AGNES: The cat died.

ARNOLPHE: What a pity! ... But to all
Things—animal, I mean—that can befall ...
Have you had rain here recently—or snow?

AGNES: No.

ARNOLPHE: Were you bored perhaps?

AGNES: I bored? Why, no.

ARNOLPHE: What have you done then in the last ten
days?

AGNES: Why, I've kept busy in a host of ways.
I made, I think, six bonnets and six slips ...

ARNOLPHE: Strange things, dear Agnes, fall from people's
lips ...

Now, just imagine—I heard Gertrude say
An elegant young man called here one day.
You suffered him to see you, heard him speak—
Made no attempt to stop him—were quite—meek
With him! ... Of course, on Gertrude's tales I set no
store.
I'd wager twenty thousand crowns and more
She's wrong ...

AGNES: Don't bet!

ARNOLPHE: Why not?

AGNES: You—wouldn't win.

ARNOLPHE: Oh ho! It's true then that a youth got in!

AGNES: Why yes! ... In fact, it happened every day—
Or almost every day you were away.

ARNOLPHE: Can I believe my ears? ... You mean a
   man? ...

AGNES: Came to this house? He did. Of that I can
   Assure you. He came often ... I could swear
   That only seldom was this youth elsewhere.

ARNOLPHE: (*aside*) With utter frankness she admits her
                                    fault.
   Perhaps after all she's suffered no assault ...
   (*to Agnes*) Hmm ... let me see ... Now, Agnes, am I right
   In saying that I bade you shun the sight
   Of strangers?

AGNES: Why of course.

ARNOLPHE: Then tell me why—

AGNES: Why, you'd have acted just the same as I!
   This youth was—different ... Why, I had no choice
   Right from the moment when I heard his voice ...
   But you are bored perhaps?

ARNOLPHE: (*frothing*)   I bored? Why no!
   (*aside*) A plague on you! (to Agnes) I simply want to
                                 know
   What happened.

AGNES: I'll proceed without delay.
   On Friday ... yes ... no, it was Saturday ...

ARNOLPHE: Who cares! Get on!

AGNES: Did you not want the truth?

ARNOLPHE: *(aside)* She certainly is dumb enough,
                                         forsooth!

AGNES: Right up there on the balcony I was sitting,
Devoting my attention to my knitting—
When right beneath me in the avenue
This elegant young man came into view ...

ARNOLPHE: If by your work you were so occupied,
How did it happen that this wretch you spied?

AGNES: *That's* easy to explain ...

ARNOLPHE: All right, don't bother!
(aside) Maybe I'll still forsake her for another!

AGNES: Well then, when this fair youth set eyes on me,
For some strange reason he showed signs of glee.
Without a word he bowed right to the ground ...
Knowing not what to do, without a sound,
I—wanting to appear at least polite—
Returned his bow ... I hope that was all right?

ARNOLPHE: Grrrrrrrr!

AGNES: Whereat he bowed again. I rebowed too.
That seemed to me the proper thing to do.
He bowed a third time—this polite young man.
I did so too. I thought—why, what I can
I'll do ... And so, while he kept bowing, I—
Fearing he'd deem me not well-bred—did try
To outbow this youth whose bowing had no flaw ...
And by nightfall I may have scored a draw!

ARNOLPHE: Continue, please ... (*aside*) I'm fearful of the
                                                          end
 Of her relations with so false a friend!

AGNES: Well, the next day there came to our front door
 An aged crone I'd never seen before.
 "Bless you, my child," she said. "God keep you fair,
 But render you compassionate too. Spare
 This innocent young man you've wounded sore!"

ARNOLPHE: Damned daughter of the devil!!

AGNES: Sir, you swore! ...
 "*I* wounded him? ... *I* wouldn't harm a flea!
 (If only *they* could say the same of me!)"
 "Oh, but you did! He's deathly sick!" she said.
 "Did I perchance drop something on his head?"
 I asked ... She said, "My precious, you *are* slow!
 It was your eyes that dealt the fatal blow!" ...
 You could have knocked me over with a feather! ...
 Well, on we talked for half an hour together.
 She said, "Some poison which you don't suspect
 Lurks in your eyes and has this sad effect.
 Unless you help this fine young man get over
 His malady, I fear he won't recover."
 "Goodness!" said I, "His death would give me pain!
 What can I do to make him well again?"
 "Why, all the young man asks of you's a trifle—
 To see you ... Yes, you make a pretty eyeful,
 I must admit ... The sight of you, he's sure,

Which made him sick, would likewise be the cure."
"Well then," I said—just what else *could* I say?—
"You'd better send him here without delay."

ARNOLPHE: (*beneath his breath*)
The cursed witch—corrupter of the young!
High on a cross in hell I'll see her hung!

AGNES: And so he came, he saw—and soon was cured!—
His suffering I couldn't have endured.—
Could I, who shrink to hear a kitten cry,
Sit quietly by and see this young man die?

ARNOLPHE: (*aside*)   Her conduct is not sinful in her eyes,
It's true ... I've been to blame! I was unwise—
Nay, guilty—to expose her innocence,
Leaving her ten long days without defence ...
Ah ha! this scapegrace, whom the devil sent
Hither ... I wonder just how far he went!

AGNES: But you're upset ... I wish you'd tell me why ...
I didn't do anything amiss, did I?

ARNOLPHE: Well, no—Well—I'd know better if you'd
                                                        tell
Exactly what you did to make him well.

AGNES: He *looked* at me—that's all ... got so excited
His ailment disappeared ... I was delighted!
He bought me a delicious Easter bonnet
With roses and carnations broidered on it,
And was so nice to Allan and Georgette—
The memory of his kindness lingers yet ...

ARNOLPHE: That's fine ... But when you two were left
alone ...?

AGNES: Oh, then he said he hoped I'd be his own
Forever—swore he'd never love again ...
Assured me he was happiest of men ...
Said he adored me ... wondered why on earth
I was so sweet to one so little worth ...
And other things too numerous to mention
Sprang tenderly from his lovesick invention ...

ARNOLPHE: (aside) Why did I start this cross-examina-
tion!
All it can lead to is my own damnation!
(to Agnes) But when he'd fully praised your loveliness,
Did this young man not give you—a caress?

AGNES: Oh yes! When he had lauded all my charms,
A hundred times he kissed my hands and arms.

ARNOLPHE: And that was all?—that is—he took no
more?

AGNES: Why no ... my hands and arms ... I said before—
(She suddenly looks guilty. He fears the worst!)

ARNOLPHE: I knew it!

AGNES: He—

ARNOLPHE: Speak up!

AGNES: I just don't dare—
You'll be so angry ...

ARNOLPHE: No I won't ...

AGNES: Then swear!

ARNOLPHE: I swear ... Now tell me ... Just what did he
take??

AGNES: The way you're looking fairly makes me quake!
He ... took ....

ARNOLPHE: Well, *out* with it!

AGNES: That ribbon gay
You gave me on my very last birthday!
I'm ... sorry .....

ARNOLPHE: Damn the ribbon! Was that all
He took? ... And did? ... That—absolutely all???

AGNES: That's all ... Besides, what else is there to do? ...

ARNOLPHE: Nothing, of course ... That's absolutely true ...
But ... come now, Agnes ... tell me ... Are you sure
He didn't perhaps suggest some other cure?

AGNES: (*trying hard to remember*)
No ... I don't think he did ... I'd have been glad,
Of course, to give him everything I had!

ARNOLPHE: (*aside*) Why, heaven be praised! I'm lightly
out of this!
With one so simple, though, how could he miss?
(*to Agnes*) Agnes, you're good, but—you must understand
'Twas wrong to let this young man kiss your hand
And so forth ... All the rascal had in mind
Was—love you and leave you. *That's* what he
designed!

AGNES: Oh, not at all! He said so ... gave his word! ...

ARNOLPHE: And you believed him? ... Agnes, you're
absurd!
Returning smiles, I'll have you know, my dear,
Accepting gifts, lending a ready ear
To all the amorous talk of these young fops—
Until at last your drowsy virtue drops
Like a ripe peach into their lecherous lap—
Is for a good girl more than a mere mishap...
It's conduct most displeasing in heaven's eyes—
A sin, in short, of quite enormous size!

AGNES: I don't see why—and I would like to know!

ARNOLPHE: Officially it's been stated to be so.

AGNES: It seems to me you still haven't told me why.

ARNOLPHE: It makes God angry—that we can't deny.

AGNES: Why it should make God angry I don't see.
I think instead he should be glad's can be!
Why, it's a most delightful thing to do! ...
(pouting)   And I knew nothing of it—thanks to you!

ARNOLPHE: Well, I'll admit that words—even deeds of
love
Are sometimes pleasing to the powers above.
They have pronounced, in fact, true love and marriage
Linked indissolubly like horse and carriage.
You can't conceive of one without the other ...
Remember this and then you'll have no bother!

AGNES: (*pondering*) If you're not married, it's a sin—
you're sure?

Married—those sinful kisses are all pure?

ARNOLPHE: Precisely.

AGNES: Unwed—love's a foul disease—

But once you're wed, you can do all you please??

ARNOLPHE: Of course!

AGNES: *Then marry me without delay!*

ARNOLPHE: (*overjoyed*) Why, Agnes! ... I shall hasten to
obey!

It was in fact this purpose brought me here!

AGNES: Impossible!

ARNOLPHE: It's true!

AGNES: Why, you're a dear!

Then we'll be wed?

ARNOLPHE: Yes, yes!

AGNES: But when?

ARNOLPHE: Tonight!

AGNES: Tonight? ... Come now! ...

ARNOLPHE: I mean it!

AGNES: Honor bright?

ARNOLPHE: My aim has always been to give you pleasure!
(*aside*) I love this girl!! Good heavens, what a treasure!

AGNES: Then let me say—whatever you may do,

Endless will be my gratitude to you! ...
Endless—no less—my heart's delight with him!

ARNOLPHE: *With whom???*

AGNES: (*faintly!*)   With—him ...

ARNOLPHE: I find *his* chances slim!!!
I've got another mate for you, you minx!
Take *me*—or stay unwed till Paris sinks!
As for your precious Mister *him*—I say
I'll be content to see you waste away
For love of him, and perish—but you'll not
Be wife of his, I tell you—though you rot!
Now, when he comes to flatter, as before,
Open a window this time—not the door!
Bid him begone! Hurl at the rascal's skull
The biggest rock that you can find, you trull!
You hear me? ... And don't count on getting by
With any trick! ... I will be there to spy!

AGNES: (*sobbing*) He was so handsome ...

ARNOLPHE: Drive him from your mind!

AGNES: I can't ... I love him!

ARNOLPHE: Silence! Or you'll find
Me harsher than you thought! ... Up to your room!

AGNES: Where you are sending me is to the tomb!

ARNOLPHE: Up to your room! And this time see you stay!
In this house *I* give orders—*you* obey!

ACT THREE

*(Arnolphe's plan to have Agnes,
Allan and Georgette repulse Horace
has apparently succeeded, and he is triumphant.)*

ARNOLPHE: Yes, you discomfited this young Don Juan!
This time at least you foiled his sordid plan—
And I forgive you for your previous folly!

GEORGETTE: Oh thank you, master!

ALLAN: Yes, we too feel jolly!

ARNOLPHE: Agnes, you're far too innocent a damsel
To venture forth without judicious counsel.
Were I not there to work out your salvation,
You were already hell-bent for damnation! ...
Don't think you can defeat this gallant's guile,
My dear, armed only with your guileless smile!
These "friendly" fellows are your bitterest foes—
Their feathers, ribbons—all their furbelows—
Feebly disguise the devil's cloven hoof
That lurks beneath! ... Once more I've furnished
   proof! ...
They're hunters—and the female heart's their prey.

35

This time, thank God, you held the hound at bay!
That rock you hurled, Agnes, dashed his hope—
With such rude tactics it is hard to cope!
That blow convinced me too we should be heading
Straight down the highway to an early wedding! ...
You're not quite ready for that yet, of course,
So I'll embark upon a short discourse
Which you'll find advantageous, I believe ...
Come, take a seat, my love. And, with your leave,
I will sit here ... If I catch you, Georgette! ...

GEORGETTE: Ah, that last scolding we will not forget,
I'll warrant! ... As for that young gentleman—
Let him fool me and Allan if he can!

ALLAN: If he gets in, I'll say goodbye to drink! ...
Besides, he's just plain stupid! What did he think?
Giving us crowns that weren't the proper weight!

ARNOLPHE: Buy something choice for supper! Then go
wait
Down at the lawyer's. Bid him come this way.
I'll have that marriage contract drawn up today!

(*Exeunt Allan and Georgette*)

Leave your work, Agnes, for a moment, dear!
Raise your head! Look at me! ... And hear! ...
Remember, too, I'll shortly ascertain
How much you will have managed to retain.

AGNES: Yes sir.

ARNOLPHE: Married to me, a hundred times a day
    You'll bless the fate that placed you in my way.
    For it was I who made you swiftly pass
    From serfdom to the upper middle class.—
    I who refused a score of marvelous matches—
    Selected you—a thing of shreds and patches—
    Reserved my couch and manly fire for *you!* ...
    You understand me, Agnes?

AGNES: Yes, I do.

ARNOLPHE: Then you must realize the only attitude
    That's possible for you is—gratitude—
    Gratitude soaring to the highest star! ...
    Just think of what you were—and what you are! ...
    I trust I make myself quite clear?

AGNES: Oh yes.

ARNOLPHE: Then clearly it behooves you to address
    Yourself to the performance of your task,
    Which henceforth will be all you ought to ask.
    For marriage stands for duty—not delight,
    In those wise women's eyes who see it right.
    Two partners join to form this blessed state—
    One is supreme, and one subordinate ...
    Here's the receipt for happy married life:
    One rules—the husband; one obeys—the wife ...
    You follow?

AGNES: Not so well this time, I fear.
    Just who obeys the wife is not quite clear,

ARNOLPHE: (*exasperated*)   What I said
  Was "one obeys—*dash*—the wife!"

                           (*aside*) V, X, Y, Zed!
  (*to Agnes*) The one *from* whom obedience comes is
                                      she—
  Obedience *to* the husband! ...

AGNES: Now I see.

ARNOLPHE: (*aside*)   The girl's stupidity's beyond belief!
  (*to Agnes*) The hommage which a soldier owes his
    chief—
  That's due from slave to master, child to sire—
  Can never match the sweet docility,
  The self-abasement, the humility,
  The reverence, the breathless adoration
  Wherewith a wife looks from her lowly station
  Up at her husband! ... Should a sudden frown
  Becloud his eye, what should she do? Look down!
  Her eyes must not seek his unless perchance
  He grants the favor of a gracious glance ...
  These lessons modern women have forgot.
  Shun all such creatures, I command! Be not
  One of those bawds of whom the whole town talks—
  Who sally forth clad in indecent frocks,
  And simper when licentious gallants leer.
  All proper self-respecting persons jeer
  Both at the frivolous woman and her mate.
  And well they know what richly merited fate

Awaits her! Through eternity she'll boil
In seething cauldrons of ebullient oil! ...
Now what I'm telling you is gospel truth.
Doubt—and 'twill be worse for you, forsooth! ...
Virtuous, your soul will be all lily-white.
Vicious, it will be black as Arctic night,
And devils, scarcely waiting for your knell,
Will drive you off to—to—*you* say it! ... Well?

(*He pauses for poor Agnes to say it, but poor Agnes is nodding.*)

Agnes! ... Good God, the girl's asleep! ...
(*But Agnes is now awake, and she catches on fast!*)

AGNES: No! Hell!
See, I *was* listening! ... "Drive you off to hell!"

ARNOLPHE: (*menacing*) I tell you you'll be damned beyond redemption
Unless you give me your complete attention!
D'ye hear?

AGNES: I do.

ARNOLPHE: God save you from your fate,
You thoughtless child, before it is too late! ...
Now that your life of service has begun,
You will be as submissive as a nun.
These, then, will be your duties ... Take and read.

(*He hands her a pamphlet*)

This is the only literature you'll need.

And see you read in clear and cheerful voice!
No husband wants a wife who doesn't rejoice!

AGNES: (*reading*)   A Guide for Wives—Maxim One
                  "Upon your wedding day,
                  Here is what you must say:
                  Though other wives may stray,
                  My husband I'll obey,
And from all other men I'll keep away."

ARNOLPHE: I shall speak further on this theme to you.
But now you may proceed to Maxim Two.

AGNES: "The choice of what you wear
                  Should be your husband's care.
If your appearance gives your spouse delight,
Who cares if others think you look a fright?"

ARNOLPHE: Sound sentiments! And I trust you agree!

AGNES: With your permission, here is Maxim Three.

          "Steer clear of perfumes, powder, lotions,
And all things that might give a lover notions!"

Husbands might well enjoy these things even more,
It seems to me.

ARNOLPHE: Pass on to Number Four!

AGNES: "The things that you find most delicious
                  Often turn out to be most pernicious.
                  So when these foolish fops start to flatter,
                  You must turn a deaf ear to their chatter!"

ARNOLPHE: To keep this maxim you must daily strive.

AGNES: I'll try. This brings us now to Number Five.
         "Be careful how you use your eyes!
         Their luster you must supervise.
         Every wife well-bred and wise
         Knows when eyes sparkle, virtue flies."

ARNOLPHE: Some shameless women claim their eyes play
                                                    tricks

    On them! Deceitful nonsense! ... Number Six!

AGNES: "Most men, when with love's flame they burn
         Are generous.
         Forget not what they yearn for in return
         From poor, weak us!"

ARNOLPHE: And when you're tempted, pray for strength
    to heaven!

AGNES: Thank you, I will ... And now for Maxim Seven.
         "In madam's boudoir there should be
         No pencil, pen, nor paper.
         Such articles have been the cause
         Of many a wifely caper.
         If madam would write *quelque chose*,
         Let it be under monsieur's nose!"

ARNOLPHE: Yes, that reminds me ... But it's getting late.
    So just pass on now, please, to Maxim Eight.

AGNES: "Wives love to meet to talk of matters
         Concerning only them.
         Husbands, who're always torn to tatters,
         Such meetings should condemn."

ARNOLPHE: I should! I will! That one's for me—not you!

AGNES: Maxim Nine.

ARNOLPHE: There's something I must do
  Before this lawyer that I've hired appears.
  My love, I haven't felt so gay in years! ...
  I won't be long! Just take another look
  Through the enchanting pages of this book!

(*Agnes retires to do as she has been told, and Arnolphe soliloquizes*)

  I can't do better than make her my wife!
  Once she is mine, she will be mine for life.
  She'll rush to execute all my commands.
  Why, she'll be like putty in my hands! ...
  I nearly lost the wench the other day,
  It's true, when like a fool I stayed away ...
  Some might contend—not wholly without sense—
  She suffers from excessive innocence.
  All I know is—if I were given the choice,
  I'd be a deal more ready to rejoice
  If she were over-dense than over-bright!
  The bright ones make you lie awake at night!...
  I've always held—and practice what I preach—
  To teach is easier far than to unteach.
  And here's advice of which no ill can come—
  If you'd keep woman docile, keep her dumb!
  Even though she's strayed a moment from the track,
  A word will bring her penitently back...

Ah, but your smart one's quite another dish—
Does what *she* wishes—never what *you* wish!
At all your time-proved maxims she will mock—
Dismiss your wisest saws as idle talk.
Vice is for her plain virtue—virtue, vice.
She'll be contriving many a shrewd device
To get her way—yes, and she'll lay the blame
On *you* if you're both buried deep in shame! ...
I'll see at least this coxcomb will not brag
That he's got Agnes' virtue in the bag!
That wagging tongue of his wrought his undoing!
It surely put a swift end to his wooing!...
Just like the Frenchmen—vain as a peacock—
Of every petty conquest they must talk!
Dull—deafening—endless their harangue—
Rather than hold their peace, the fools would hang!...
A woman must be really bent on sin
To tolerate their silly, senseless din!...

(*He spies Horace.*)

Here comes a sample!... My, he's looking grim!
Let's get the gory details out of him!

HORACE: Since I disclosed the contents of my heart,
Things have occurred, egad, that made me smart!

ARNOLPHE: Come, you don't say! I don't believe a word.

HORACE: It's all too true—and utterly absurd! ...
The girl's sour patron—by an ill-starred fate—
Came just before—for him—it was too late!

ARNOLPHE: Too bad!

HORACE: Too bad indeed! And, sad to say,
   Somehow got wind of what was under way
   Betwixt the damsel and myself!

ARNOLPHE: Well, well!

HORACE: So now for us will ring no wedding bell!

ARNOLPHE: How did he do it?

HORACE: I'd tell you if I could.

ARNOLPHE: He must be diabolically shrewd!

HORACE: The method he employed, alas, is hid
   From me. All I can say is that he did.
   Reaching my angel's house just yesterday,
   Both maid and pompous butler bar my way—
   Their countenance not smiling, but severe.
   Grimly they challenge me: "What want you here?"
   And while I pause, debating how to treat
   Their insolence, they thrust me into the street!

ARNOLPHE: (*trying in vain to conceal his delight at Horace's discomfiture*)
   Into the street, you say? Ha, ha!
   (*remembering himself*)   The clowns!

HORACE: Their impudence, I tell you, passed all bounds!

ARNOLPHE: They didn't admit you, then?

HORACE: Admit me? No!
   And darling Agnes dealt the final blow
   To my fond hopes—for "Master's back," she said.

"Be off! Begone!"—And hurled square at my head
A rock!

ARNOLPHE: A rock?

HORACE: Of no minute dimensions!
That shows you how she welcomed *my* attentions!

ARNOLPHE: Well now—that really put you in your place!
You're going to be the loser in this race.

HORACE: I fear I am indeed ... Ah, I'm so sad
To think ....

ARNOLPHE: Me too! ... *it's just ... too ... bad!*

HORACE: This surly rascal has completely foiled
My plan!

ARNOLPHE: I fear he has.

HORACE: Eqad! He's spoiled
Everything!

ARNOLPHE: My heart *does* bleed for you! ...
But courage! ... Though the prospect's bleak, it's true,
I have a feeling that you'll still make out.

HORACE: You do?

ARNOLPHE: I really do—beyond a doubt ...
Perhaps the girl still loves you after all.

HORACE: Of that, of course, there is no doubt at all.

ARNOLPHE: *What did you say??*

HORACE: Oh, I forgot to mention—
Agnes displayed remarkable invention—

You may be even more amazed than I,
Hearing how one so ignorant and shy
All of a sudden became cunning—bold—
Repaid her crafty tyrant fifty-fold!
Who'd have suspected one devoid of guile
Of fabricating such an artful wile!

ARNOLPHE: What do you mean? ... I'm all confused ...
    I bid
You tell me now exactly what she did!

HORACE: Ah, sir, this love—this wonder-working love—
Where can it come from but from heaven above!
Deep-buried riches it brings up to view!

ARNOLPHE: (*alarmed*)   No riddles, please! ... What did
    the hussy do? ...

HORACE: I'll tell you. (*But he is in no hurry*)
                    And I feel it could occur
To your good self as easily as to her ...
There is no limit to this Cupid's art—
The plain grow handsome—and the stupid, smart.
The gloomy miser's generous in a trice.
Cowards grow brave, and churlish creatures—nice! ...
Well, Love went likewise to my darling's head!
Listen! ... I think I told you what she said:
"Be off! ... Begone! ... I'll have no more to do
With an offensive character like you!"
That's what she *said* ... But that's not what she *wrote!*
Firmly attached to that rock was a note!

ARNOLPHE: A note???

HORACE: That would make any lover gay! ...
Aren't you amazed?

ARNOLPHE: *I am!* What did it say?

HORACE: It's confidential—but since you're my friend,
I think I'll let you hear it ... Please attend—
For though the girl deplores her lack of art,
I swear her simple words will melt your heart!

ARNOLPHE: Here's the result of teaching her to write! ...
Upon these nuns I'll swiftly vent my spite!

(*Horace reads the letter*)

"Kind sir, I'm at a loss where to begin—
And I do hope that writing you's no sin.
I realize, alas, I'm far from smart,
And what I say will not be said with art.
But I can't live unless I let you know
That for some reason my poor heart says *no*
When I am bidden to drive you away.
You are the one with whom I want to stay
Forever! ... I've been told young men deceive,
But somehow I can't make myself believe
You would betray me ... Tell me you're sincere
Again—again! Tell me I've naught to fear!
For if all you have sworn should prove a lie,
I verily believe that I should die."

No, Agnes, no! You've naught to fear from me!

(*to Arnolphe*) She's an amazing girl—don't you agree!

ARNOLPHE: (*aside*) Curses!

HORACE: And don't you marvel at her wit!
Why, bless me! I can't stop admiring it! ...
And don't you laugh to think the wretch who schooled
Her should turn out to be the one that's fooled! ...
Well, *don't* you! ...

ARNOLPHE: (*doing his best*) Yes ... indeed I ... do.

HORACE: (*not yet satisfied*) Well—*do!!*

ARNOLPHE: I fear I ... haven't as ... loud a laugh as you.

HORACE: (*exulting*) This boor who fortified his house
with rocks
And paving stones—no less—and armed his flocks
Of servants to fight off poor, harmless me!
Well—on us both he brought some misery
By turning up at such an awkward moment!
But he's proved such a ludicrous opponent—
Duped by this creature whom he thought to dupe—
I've never heard of such a nincompoop! ...
Come! Join me laughing at this foolish man!

ARNOLPHE: I tell you I am doing all I can! (*And he is!*)

HORACE: This note of hers ... How exquisitely kind!
A faithful picture of a gentle mind
Pricked for the first time by the potent dart
Of love! ... No, darling, we two'll *never* part! ...

ARNOLPHE: *(aside)* The jade!

HORACE: What?

ARNOLPHE: Nothing. *(aside)* Just wait till I get her!

HORACE: Can anyone conceive a sweeter letter!
Gracious reflection of her own sweet soul! ...
To see her languishing in the control
Of this curmudgeon makes me boil with rage!
This selfish rogue who's locked her in the cage
Of ignorance—her gentle nature marred—
Her path to life and love so cruelly barred! ...
But love has now begun to pierce the veil!
He'll find his jealousy of no avail
Against devotion such as mine! ...

ARNOLPHE: Goodby,
I must go now ...

HORACE: But, Arnolphe, tell me why ...

ARNOLPHE: I have some business ... I can say no more ...

HORACE: Arnolphe, my friend—you live almost next
door.
You must know someone who can get me in.
Do me this friendly service! It's no sin! ...
What should I hesitate to ask your aid?
I'd do the same for you ... The stupid maid
And still more stupid butler have forgot
My generosity. They can't be bought...
Then that old woman—bless the old girl's heart—

Selected just this moment to depart
This life—the one, I mean, who told my dove
I simply could not live without her love ...
What can I do? Whom can I now turn to?
I honestly can think of none but you ...
I'll leave you now, though, for you seem to be
Weary of hearing a young fool like me.

(*Exit Horace*)

ARNOLPHE: (*alone*)   Where can I hide my rage and my
     vexation?
Where flee the flame of my humiliation? ...
Where did this fickle jade pick up her wit?
Try as I may, I can't account for it ...
She who was—oh, so modest—so demure ...
The burning thought of her I can't endure!
And then that frightful letter that she wrote! ...
Ah, when the traitresss penned those lines, she smote
Me hard and deep! ... How could she? Tell me why ...
What ever but a slave for her was I?
She who had nothing—didn't I give her all!
I'd have lived happy at her beck and call ...
I obeyed reason wanting her as bride—
But it's not reason—now she's left my side—
That aches to taste the rapture of her charms,
Destined to lie now in another's arms! ...
For she is lost—lost to this profligate ...
Shall I entrust his punishment to fate?

Or strike him down and follow him to hell? ...
Perhaps for all three of us now tolls the bell ...
I love her still! ... Not theirs—but mine the blame!
I'm like to burst with rage and spite and shame!
I hate and hunger for her! ... I've no choice—
I needs must be where I can hear her voice ...
I needs must go and study for a space
The print of perfidy upon her face!

ACT FOUR

*(In the interval between the acts,
Arnolphe has seen Agnes)*

ARNOLPHE: I wouldn't have believed it! ... There she
    stood
Calm as a statue carved of antique wood! ...
Confronted with a smile so bright—so bland,
Who would have ever dreamed she'd had a hand
In this foul plot which may cost me my mind! ...
Deceit—thy name indeed is womankind!
And yet the more I grieved and stormed and hated
(Are men *predestined* to be addlepated?)
More beauteous she grew! And all the more
I ached for her as ne'er I'd ached before! ...
Oh, shame on me! If she escapes me now,
After long years devoted to endow
Her with the virtues of a perfect wife,
I'll lose not only her—I'll lose my *life!* ...
But I'll *not* lose her! ... I'll let no young fool
Steal the first fruits of years of patient rule! ...
She's fallen half in love with him, may be—
But she's at least three-quarters wed to me!

And she'll be wholly wed by set of sun.

It's high time this tomfoolery were done!

(*Enter the Lawyer. The humor of this short scene lies in the fact that the lawyer thinks Arnolphe is answering him, whereas Arnolphe is ignorant of his presence and is simply soliloquizing.*)

LAWYER: Ah, here he is!... How are you, sir?... You see I've come to do what you desired of me.

ARNOLPHE: But how's it to be done?

LAWYER: The usual way.

ARNOLPHE: I should proceed with caution, I daresay ...

LAWYER: You can have every confidence in me ...

ARNOLPHE: Can I place trust in such a one as she? ...

LAWYER: Until the dowry's paid, simply don't sign ...
Don't worry, sir! I'll make your interests mine!

ARNOLPHE: Suppose I bring it to the light of day?
Then comes the question: What will people say? ...

LAWYER: On that score you can set your mind at ease ...
We'll keep the contract secret, if you please ...

ARNOLPHE: I love her! That's the root of all my woe!

LAWYER: Then you can settle more on her, you know ...

ARNOLPHE: Just how should I behave on this occasion?

LAWYER: I see no earthly reason for evasion.
Her dowry's one third hers—so says the law.
But a good lawyer always finds a flaw ...

Once I have found it—and you've paid my bill—
You can do with her dowry what you will.

ARNOLPHE: If I—

LAWYER: Consult with her if you prefer,
But to your wishes she must needs defer!

ARNOLPHE: (*finally seeing the lawyer*)
What's that??

LAWYER: What you will do, you see, depends
On what you reckon will best serve your ends.
You may bequeath her your entire estate,
Which will, of course, if she dies intestate,
Pass upon her decease with what accrues
From *bona fide* sale of chattels, if you choose,
To her male heirs in usufruct till death—
Heredes eius—as the statute saith—
Who once the aforesaid will has been probated,
And proof presented they're indeed related ...
Why are you staring? ... Think you I'm a fool??
My specialty is contracts! ... My head's full
Of *quam ob rems, ius primae noctis, sui* ...

ARNOLPHE: No doubt! ... But just who cares for all this
    hooey!

LAWYER: (*foaming*) *You* do! ... You must! ... Twas
    you who sent for me.
    (*aside*) He's lost his reason—that's not hard to see!

ARNOLPHE: There *was* a marriage contract in the plans,

But it's too early yet to post the banns ...
Come, quit your jabbering and be on your way!

LAWYER: Your courtesy enchants me, I must say!

ARNOLPHE: Plague take this fellow with his puppy face!...
Be off! Or else get ready for the chase!

(*Exit Arnolphe. Enter Allan and Georgette*)

LAWYER: Now, *did* your master send you to fetch me?

ALLAN: Yessir, he did. Of that right sure I be.

LAWYER: Then tell me—do you think your master's sane?

ALLAN: Since *I*'m not mad, I feel I should refrain
From saying *no* ... But I can't tell a lie.

LAWYER: On one thing we agree then—you and I ...
Tell him from me he is a first-class *fool!*

GEORGETTE: From *you*, we will!

ALLAN: Count on us!... As a rule
He's here around this hour ... (*Exit Lawyer*) Yes, here
He comes ... Oh, master...hm ... it would appear
This lawyer finds ...

ARNOLPHE: I don't care what he finds! ...

GEORGETTE: Yes, but he said ...

ARNOLPHE: Get the fool off your minds!
Attend to me! (*seductive*) You're my best friends ...

BOTH: (*sceptical*) Hmmmmmmmmm!

ARNOLPHE: Don't interrupt! ... My happiness depends
On you ... Let me explain ... A wicked plot

'S been hatched, I say, to leave me not a jot
Of honor! ... Now, what would *your* feelings be
If some day your dear master you should see
Jeered at while walking down the street?

ALLAN: I would feel *awful!*

GEORGETTE: I just couldn't *eat!*

ARNOLPHE: So this is *your* affair as well as mine!
You must—no matter what he says—decline
To give the slightest aid to this young man!

ALLAN: *We* know!

GEORGETTE: We told you we'd do all we can!

ARNOLPHE: Pay no attention to a single word
He says!

ALLAN: Right!

GEORGETTE: I'll pretend I haven't heard!

ARNOLPHE: Good! ... But he's cunning ... Tell me what
   you'd say
Were he to whimper at the door today:
"Allan—dear, good, kind Allan—I'm so sad,
And only you have power to make me glad!"

ALLAN: "Sir, you're a fool!" I'd say!

ARNOLPHE: (*Continuing to impersonate Horace*) "Georgette,
   your charms are far from easy to forget!"

GEORGETTE: Sir, you're a knave!

ARNOLPHE: "I don't want you to do
A thing, Allan, that you might later rue!"

ALLAN: Sir, you're a rogue!

ARNOLPHE: Bravo! ... "Why, I may die
If I don't find in you a staunch ally!"

ALLAN: Sir, you're a dolt, an ass, a clown!

ARNOLPHE: Ah, now I know you will not let me down! ...
Let's try again—just once! ... "Georgette,
You know I'm not the sort that will forget
A service rendered ... Allan, I'll repay
Right gladly any favor that you may
See fit to do me ... Come, take this crown! (*Allan does!*)
Georgette, go buy yourself a fine new gown!

(*He offers her money too, which she accepts with gusto*)

This is the merest sample of my largess—
And all I ask from you's—a glimpse of ... Agnes!"

ALLAN: Get out!

ARNOLPHE: Bravo!

GEORGETTE: Be off!

ARNOLPHE: That's good!

ALLAN: And quick!

ARNOLPHE: Fine! (*In their zeal they nearly knock him over, however*)
But go easy, though! ... Put down that stick!!

ALLAN: That's what you want?

GEORGETTE: See! *He* won't find it funny!

ARNOLPHE: I'm sure he won't ... But don't accept his
    money!

ALLAN: I didn't think ...

GEORGETTE: I just held out my hand ...

ALLAN: Let's do't again!

ARNOLPHE: I see you understand.
    So that will do ... Go in now—both of you!

ALLAN: (*ready for more*)   Just say the word!

ARNOLPHE: No, that will be enough ...
    Be on your guard, I say! And—well—be rough
    With him if you're obliged to ... And—I say—
    Oh ... Keep the money!

ALLAN: *Thank you!*

GEORGETTE: Happy day!

                    (*Exeunt Allan and Georgette*)

ARNOLPHE: I'd trust them further if I had a spy
    To watch them ... There's a cobbler lives near by
    Who might, I think, be hired at little cost
    To see she doesn't get out—and keep a host
    Of undesirables from getting in.
    To be specific—all who snip and pin,
    Who cut and curl hair, who sell paint and scent—
    Such scum are by the very devil sent!—
    Who deal in bonnets, silks and scarves
    (No sense in doing things by halves)—
    Love's the commodity in which *they* trade

As often as their own, I have heard said.
They revel in arranging rendez-vous.
They're eager to deliver billets doux.
If he puts through a message to his flame,
I'll be quite ready to take all the blame!

(*Enter Horace, obviously agitated*)

HORACE: No! Never have I had a narrower shave!
This time my hopes were wellnigh in the grave! ...
I'll tell you all! ... As I was passing by,
Fair Agnes on the balcony I spy.
Downstairs she rushed to meet me—and before
I had my breath back, she unbarred the door.
I took her in my arms, and to her room
We sped—when suddenly the sound of doom
We heard—*his* step upon the stair! ...
Fortune had placed a spacious closet there.
In it I popped—and none too soon at that!
He stormed right in—My heart went pit-a-pat!
And as he stumbled madly to and fro,
He cursed, he groaned, delivered many a blow
At this and that—kicked her pet dog, and smashed
The flower pots on the mantle, as he dashed
From door to window and back to door again,
Swearing he was th'unluckiest of men!
He'd found out that she'd tricked him, that was clear—
And he was harried by both rage and fear
Lest all his precious honor sink in shame ...

Well, out at last he went—and out I came.
Even though her room for me was paradise,
To linger then seemed to us both unwise.
But ere I tore myself from Agnes' sight,
We planned to meet again this very night!
I am to cough beneath her window thrice.
She'll have the window open in a trice.
Then on a ladder nimbly I'll ascend
Rung after rung to *very heaven*, my friend! ...
Telling of joy in store makes the joy double—
Pardon me, then, for giving you the trouble
Of listening to a story which, 'tis true,
Can hold but little interest for you...
I'm off now. Several things must be prepared ...
Tomorrow I will tell you how we fared!

(*Exit Horace. Another soliloquy from Arnolphe*)

ARNOLPHE:　So fate sees fit to fire another blast
Before I have recovered from the last!...
Does destiny demand that I should sit
And watch my well-laid plans foiled by the wit—
Time after time—of such a witless, callow
Pair? ... A bitter pill indeed to swallow! ...
Twenty long years I've set myself to learn
How a once-happy husband comes to earn
The shameful decorations on his brow—
And I was sure I had discovered how
To keep *their* downfall from becoming mine.

I would at least have no cause to repine,
I blithely thought! By high hopes I was buoyed!
The vulgar errors *they'd* made I'd avoid! ...
So said I yesterday ... Alas, today
I share in the ubiquitous dismay ...
Does fate decree a husband's heart *must* ache
No matter what precautions he may take?
My constant prudence cannot be gainsaid—
Yet must I too submit to being betrayed?....
All's not yet lost, though! ... I still hold the prize
For which this impudent seducer sighs!
Though the young scapegrace may have stolen her heart,
I'll see to it he gets no other part
Of her! This night *they* plan to spend in joy
I plan to have them otherwise employ! ...
How droll that in this battle for survival
My weapons should be furnished by my rival!

(*Enter Chrysalde*)

CHRYSALDE: Well met, my friend! ... And all the pleasure's mine!

   I've come to take you home with me to dine.

ARNOLPHE: No thanks.

CHRYSALDE: Oh, come now!

ARNOLPHE: No, tonight I fast!

CHRYSALDE: But why? ... I promise you a choice repast!

ARNOLPHE: Too bad!

CHRYSALDE: (*teasing him*) In love perhaps you've fallen
from grace? ...
Ah, ha! I think I see it in your face! ...
So the fair Agnes proved not quite so amative?

ARNOLPHE: I'll thank you to be somewhat less inquisitive!

CHRYSALDE: Oh, don't be peevish!

ARNOLPHE: Well, if I'm betrayed,
At least I've fought against it ... I've not made
A point to show how casually I view
Her conduct—as so many husbands do!
I've not sat quietly by ... Men may deride,
But I didn't bring this lover to her side!

CHRYSALDE: I marvel seeing one so smart as you
Making of such events so much ado,
In matters where what you can do's so little,
Your honor's not involved one jot or tittle! ...
Why stake your sovereign happiness on this:
Whether it's you or he that gets the kiss? ...
Woman's a fragile thing. Why load upon her
Poor weak back the burden of *your* honor?
Just why consider *this* the only blot?

(*He mimicks Arnolphe*)

"If his wife's true, it matters not a jot
If he's a liar, coward, bully, cheat!"
I find such faulty thinking hard to beat!

ARNOLPHE: *You* think *your* way—and let *me* think *mine!*

CHRYSALDE: Why should I, when *your* thinking's out of
    line!
  The wife is vain, capricious, prone to cheat—
  Should the wronged husband, then, no longer eat?
  Can levity of hers change *his* virtue to vice? ...
  Surely the least reflection should suffice
  To show that attitude's ridiculous!
  The man of honor simply makes no fuss.
  He does not, by rejoicing, court disgrace,
  But he can find no cause to hide his face!
  Nor does he choose, by making vulgar noise,
  To tell the world just how his wife employs
  Her time ... Nor have *you* cause to make a stew
  Because *your* future wife has tired of you!

ARNOLPHE: Stop it, I say! ... I love her! ... I can't bear ...

CHRYSALDE: Because *you* love her, you think *she* should
    care?
  What makes you think that you alone are lovable?
  You surely cannot be that gullible! ...
  Her loss is matter for regret—not rage,
  Nor shame, nor hate! ... Just quietly turn the page ...
  Though the dear girl's been frail, it's not the end ...
  You've not committed murder! ... Many a friend
  Will still respect you. Why, then, rant and rave
  As though all you could hope for was the grave?

ARNOLPHE: So *you'd* advise: keep laughing and grow
    fatter—
  As though her damned delinquence didn't matter!

CHRYSALDE: Don't be a fool! ... Losing a wife's an ill—
Sometimes ... But I know things more grievous still.
I'd rather have a well-bred wife who's "human"—
And I mean "frail"—than a self-styled "honest woman"
Who vaunts her precious virtue morn till night,
And scolds and snarls at everyone in sight.
She may be lazy, stupid—but she's pure!
You pay a pretty price, though! You endure
Her clacking tongue—her coarse, ill-tempered manner ...
If I lost such a wife, I'd hoist a banner! ...
It's bad being jilted by a wife you want.
It's worse being hung on to by one you don't!

ARNOLPHE: If these are really your opinions—fine!
With your permission, though, I'll stick to mine.

CHRYSALDE: When *your* turn comes, perhaps you'll
change your mind.

ARNOLPHE: When *my* turn comes? ... That really was
unkind!

CHRYSALDE: 'Twas *you*, not I, who talked of being
betrayed ...
Your memory's going too, I am afraid!

ARNOLPHE: It hasn't happened yet ... In fact, I hope ...

CHRYSALDE: Well, if it does, this thought will help you
cope
With your vexation ... Thousands who're richer far,
And handsomer, and better born—who are
Smarter than you, in temper far more equable—

Whom *you'd* think *any* wife would think more lovable
Have met with this disaster and survived! ...
You'll find there *is* no scheme for being well-wived!

ARNOLPHE: That won't be MY fate, sir, I swear!

CHRYSALDE: Don't swear!
For men don't swear until they're halfway there!

ARNOLPHE: I swear I'll still swear! And I'll prove you
   wrong!
To ME—not HIM—this hussy will belong!

(*He runs in extreme agitation to knock at the door, and Allan
and Georgette appear. He is so upset that his next speech is almost
sincere.*)

I love you both!

GEORGETTE: Well, *this* is something new!

ARNOLPHE: And I implore your aid.

ALLAN: You really do?

ARNOLPHE: *You* love me too ... Show me how much
   this night,
   Georgette!

GEORGETTE: (*misunderstanding*)   Oh master! ...

ALLAN: (*reproachful*)   You've given her a fright.

ARNOLPHE: Listen, you fools, I love you! Damn you both!
And *I'm* prepared to show you I'm not loth
To give you proof in florins, ducats, guineas—
So please stop acting like a pair of ninnies!

ALLAN: We understand.

GEORGETTE: You've been so pleased with us
    You feel you should have been more generous.

ARNOLPHE: Listen! ... Tonight, on his foul purpose bent,
    This youth to Agnes' room plans an ascent.
    We three, however, will be there to see
    He doesn't get to where he longs to be.
    You'll lie in wait, each brandishing a stick—
    It's up to you to say how long, how thick!—
    And when he's reached the last rung of the ladder—
    Ready to dart at Agnes like an adder,
    I'll ope the window—*you'll* proceed to shower
    Blows on his back he'll nurse for many an hour! ...
    But make no mention, mind you, of *my* name,
    Nor say I'm there! ... You two will take the blame ...
    Now, are you brave enough? Or do you shrink?

GEORGETTE: I see no danger.

ALLAN: Come now, master—think!
    What should *we* fear so long as *he's* no stick
    To strike us with!

GEORGETTE: This is the lastest trick
    He'll play on you! ... Oh my, won't this be fun!

ARNOLPHE: Be off! ... I'll see you when the battle's won!

                                        (*Exeunt*)

    If all you husbands who don't sleep at night
    Because your wives are not behaving right
    Were to receive their paramours like *this*,
    Soon you'd be back again in wedded bliss!

ACT FIVE

ARNOLPHE: (*furious*) I said, "Be bold!"—but *you* were
  overbold!

GEORGETTE and ALLAN (*puzzled*)
  We didn't do a thing we weren't told!

ARNOLPHE: I said to make him *sore*—not make him
  dead!
  I told you—"Hit the back!" *You* hit the head!
  You've murdered him! ... This will go hard indeed
  With you! ... I fear you'll swing for this foul deed ...
  Remember, please, when your neck's in the noose,
  Don't find in my—suggestion an excuse! ...
  Of course, I've no objection if you say
  I said you might, perhaps, *frighten* him away.

ALLAN: Alack, I can't remember what you said.

GEORGETTE: We did it, though! I know! ...

ARNOLPHE: Get off to bed!
                                          (*Exeunt in haste*)

  It's almost daybreak ... When I've had some rest,
  I'll be more able to decide what's best ...
  A hundred things occur to me I'd rather
  Do than break this bad news to his poor father.
                    (*Enter Horace—bloody but unbowed*)

HORACE: Who's there? ... Now, who can be abroad so
late?

ARNOLPHE: (*neither seeing nor hearing Horace yet*)
I never dreamed the fools would smash his pate ...
(*He sees Horace*) Who's there? ... It's *you?* ... Yes, but it
can't be you!

HORACE: It is ... And I'm ashamed ... I come to sue
For one more boon ... (*realizing it*) You're early out,
egad!

ARNOLPHE: Can this be witchcraft? ... Am I going mad?

HORACE: You simply won't believe what I've been
through!

ARNOLPHE: Well, I don't quite—but still I'm glad it's
you! ...
I don't know what you've come to ask, my boy,
But that you're here to ask it gives me joy!

HORACE: Everything's gone marvelously well
With me! ... But I've the strangest tale to tell!
You'll see how I've been flirting with disaster ...
I formed a plan which would have got me past her
Cantankerous jailer up to her dear room,
Which *I*'d have made a deal less like a tomb!
But he, somehow, learned what was under way
(Some traitor must have given me away).
As I reached up to grab her window-sill,
A band of rogues bore down on me to kill
Me. But before they struck—why, down I fell

To earth—and so escaped, you see, to tell
My tale!

ARNOLPHE: I see ... You're *quite* sure you're alive?

HORACE: At least as sure as that the clock's struck five! ...
Though I was bruised, at least I wasn't battered,
And at the moment that was all that mattered!

ARNOLPHE: You weren't really hurt?

HORACE: By luck I was!—
I say "by luck"—for pain forced me to pause
A while there, prostrate on the ground.
Eventually my enemies came around
(I'm pretty sure my special foe was one ...
'Twas he, no doubt, who organized the fun.)
They saw me motionless and thought me dead.
"Drat him! cried one, "His blood is on our head!"
I can assure you they made quite a pother,
Each shooting off reproaches at the other,
And cursing me, and prodding with their sticks.
(Thank St. Jerome the night was black as Styx!)
At last they left—their hearts filled with dismay ...
I was about to make my get-away,
When I beheld fair Agnes at my side! ...

ARNOLPHE: (*in spite of himself*) Her door was locked!

HORACE: (*not catching on*) They left it gaping wide
When they rushed headlong down the stair ...
You should have seen the poor girl tear her hair
When she spied me, all bloody, lying there!

To cut my story—such was her delight
On finding me not dead—but quite all right—
She put her foot down, tossed her pretty head,
And roundly swore she wouldn't go back to bed
Unless I came along!

ARNOLPHE: Where is she now?

HORACE: That's what I'm coming to—if you'll allow! ...
I trust you see how this man void of sense
Might well have made her lose her innocence! ...
For Agnes I've, of course, so much respect
That I was forced her offer to reject.

ARNOLPHE: (*relieved*)   Yes, you did well! ... But still I fail
                                                   to see
Exactly what boon you desire of me.

HORACE: I hoped you'd ... let me turn her over to you ...
Oh, not for long! ... Just for a day or two ...

ARNOLPHE: (*Ah!*)   Please say no more! I grant your
    wish with pleasure!
Fear not, I'll keep a close eye on your treasure.

HORACE: A thousand thanks, Arnolphe! ... You see, I'd
    rather
She'd stay right here while I talk with her father
About our marriage ... This Zouche will pursue
Her, and I'd love to know she's safe with you.

ARNOLPHE: I can refuse you nothing ... Simply ask!
Besides, it should prove quite a pleasant task.

HORACE: She'll cause no trouble—that I guarantee!
   You'll be amazed to see how sweet she'll be! ...
   I only hope you won't feel I've abused
   Your kindness ... That fear leaves me quite confused.

ARNOLPHE: My friend, even though you had not made
      the offer,
   I'd have *suggested* that you turn her over!
   But how should we proceed? ... It's almost dawn
   We want no busy bodies looking on
   When you entrust fair Agnes to my care ...
   My front door gives out on the street.
   To bring her there would be quite indiscreet ...
   Let's say this corner near my garden gate.
   It's darker there ... There then is where I'll wait.

HORACE: Splendid! We'll have no reason for delay ...
   I'll hand her over and be on my way!

(*He goes off to fetch Agnes and Arnolphe goes over to the garden,
which is plunged in shadow*)

ARNOLPHE: If I reviled you, Fate, I take it back!
   Give me this girl—and *nothing* I will lack!

             (*Re-enter Horace, leading a reluctant Agnes*)

HORACE: Trust me, my darling ... You poor, homeless
      waif—
   Where I am taking you, you will be safe!
   We can't yet live together, you and I.
   Someday, when I'm less rushed, I'll tell you why!

AGNES: Ah, *must* you leave me?

HORACE: Agnes, dear, I must!

AGNES: All our fond hopes are lying in the dust!
  I'll know no happiness till you return.

HORACE: For you each moment I will fondly yearn!

AGNES: Always, when we're apart, I will be sad.

HORACE: When you have left my side, I'm never glad ...

AGNES: Then all you have to do, my love, is stay!

HORACE: I'd love to be with you day after day!—
  And—do believe me—if I could, I would!

AGNES: It seems to me that if you would, you could ...
  But this man's pulling me ...

HORACE: He's my best friend.
  The future of our love may well depend
  On him ... He'll see to it that we're not seen.

AGNES: But he's a stranger—and you know I've been
  Brought up to frown on strangers—specially men!

HORACE: Come, my love, there's a gulf twixt now and
      then! ...
  Fear nothing ... In his hands you'll rest secure!

AGNES: I'd prefer yours. Of that you can be sure!

HORACE: Farewell!

AGNES: Already? Please don't leave me yet!

HORACE: I must! The day is breaking. Don't forget
  I'm yours forever ... I'll be back before
  You've missed me!

AGNES: No, my heart's already sore!

HORACE: My love! (*As he exits*) I swear I never thought
   I would

   Agree that all things work together for good!

ARNOLPHE: This way, please, mademoiselle ... A few steps
   still!

   I said I'd keep you safely—and I will! ...

   (*somber*) I think we've met before ...

AGNES: Mother o' God,

   It's *him!*

ARNOLPHE: No, it's not *him*, you little bawd,

   It's *me!* ... You find me an unpleasant sight,

   If I construe your sentiments aright!

                    (*Agnes looks frantically for Horace*)

   Don't waste time looking for your silly swain!

   An age will pass before he's here again! ...

   You ask, forsooth, if children come from cabbage,

   And then, you shameful little baggage,

   You set forth gaily on an escapade

   The like of which no decent, well-bred maid

   Would dream of ...

AGNES: You forget—I'm *not* well-bred!

ARNOLPHE: Keep to the point, please! ... This impudent
                                        fool

   Has taught you things you did not learn in school!

   Now you are not afraid of ghosts, it seems...

No longer does the devil haunt your dreams!
Too bad! ... (*Change of strategy*) Oh, Agnes, what a
    shabby way
You've chosen all my kindness to repay!
The hand that fed you you've seen fit to bite ...
Oh, my betrothed—why didn't you treat me *right!*

AGNES: Quite frankly, sir, I don't know what you mean.
I see no cause for you to make a scene.

ARNOLPHE: (*sarcastic*) If someone's wrong, of course, *I*
    am the one!

AGNES: I find no wrong in anything *I*'ve done!

ARNOLPHE: Taking a lover's no disgrace, 'od's life?

AGNES: *This* lover wanted me to be his wife!
You were my teacher. I did what you said.
And you said, "It's no sin if you are wed."

ARNOLPHE: The husband, though, I planned for you
    was *I!*
I've told you so a hundred times, haven't I!

AGNES: What I've told you is every bit as true:
I'd much prefer to marry *him* than *you!*
All *you've* contrived to do is fill my head full
Of ideas about marriage I find dreadful!
But *he* paints marriage filled with rare delights
That I can't sleep for thinking of at nights!

ARNOLPHE: Because you love him, minx!

AGNES: Of course I do!

ARNOLPHE: You say that to my face, you hussy, you ...?

AGNES: I don't see why I shouldn't, if it's true!

ARNOLPHE: You had no right to love him, don't you see!

AGNES: I couldn't help it! ... Talk to *him*—not *me!*

ARNOLPHE: You should have driven this passion from your heart!

AGNES: Why? ... If I had, we'd have been forced to part!
I *can* see driving out things that annoy.
But why drive out a thing that gives you joy?

ARNOLPHE: Because you knew that it would make me furious!

AGNES: Oh no, I didn't ... Tell me why ... I'm curious.

ARNOLPHE: Oh, what's the use? ... I'm wrong, of course ... You're right!
I view your girlish passion with delight! ...
You don't love *me* then?

AGNES: *I* love *you?* Why no!

ARNOLPHE: You don't?

AGNES: *No!*

ARNOLPHE: And you dare to tell me so?

AGNES: I fail to see why not ... *I*'m not to blame.
Your chance and his to woo me were the same.
If you lost out, perhaps you just didn't try!

ARNOLPHE: Not try? ... I struggled till I thought I'd die!

AGNES: Then *he* must be more competent—that's all.
He didn't seem to have to try at all.

ARNOLPHE: You've picked up quite a gift for repartee!
The devil's had his hand in this, I see! ...
Unless a stupid wench of love knows more
Than do philosophers with all their lore...
Since, then, in logic you are SO well versed—
And all your answers apt as though rehearsed—
Answer me this: What leads you to believe
I'd board and house you just so you could leave
And marry him? ... Thirteen long years *I* pay
To behold you clope with him today!

AGNES: He'll pay you back—yes, down to the last sou!

ARNOLPHE: What of my rights? ... Will he pay THEM
back too?

AGNES: Your rights may well not be what they appear.

ARNOLPHE: Did I not educate you many a year??

AGNES: You did a grand job—that can't be denied!
You'd have done better if you hadn't tried!
I've no illusions ... I can't take a bow.
I'm no more educated than a cow!
I'm heartily ashamed ... And I will not
Stand any longer for it. See? ... That's what!

ARNOLPHE: And so you took this ignorant young colt
For your instructor! ... Dolt thus teaches dolt!

AGNES: At least he's taught me everything I know ...
A great deal more to HIM than YOU I owe!

ARNOLPHE: What I should do as well as scold you roundly

For your impertinence is—*Smack you soundly!*
The best cure for your insolence, my dear,
Would be for me to up and *box your ear!*

AGNES: (*the minx!*)   Why not? ... If that affords you satis-
faction?

ARNOLPHE: (*aside*)   Confound the wench! ... I can't take
proper action! ...
Now she's become so meek, she's quite disarming.
Curse her whole sex, I say, for being so charming!
The only thing these helpless creatures can
Accomplish is the snaring of a man! ...
They don't possess a single decent quality...
In only one trait they excel—frivolity!
Yet there is nothing anyone can name
That comes within a mile of being the same ...
(*to Agnes*) Well, I surrender ... You're the one to score!
You're pardoned ... And I love you as before ...
Now that you've seen th'extent of my affection,
You'll surely send *some* love in my direction!

AGNES: Why, I'd be glad to love you if I could.
But somehow I just can't get in the mood.

ARNOLPHE: I'm sure you could if you would only try.
Just listen! (*He sighs*) Wasn't that a whopping sigh!
I can as easily die of love as he! ...
Quit the young scamp! Throw in your lot with me! ...
You were bewitched ... When you're yourself again,
You'll marvel how you thought *him* best of men!

I swear you will be merrier with me
A hundred times than you could hope to be
With him ... And you love merriment, I know ...
And you enjoy being spoiled, too, isn't that so!
Well, *I*'ll hug, kiss, caress you day and night.
Our life will be just one long amorous fight!
I'll let you do exactly as you please—
No questions asked! (*aside*) *I*'ve caught this dread
   disease!
(*to her*) Until today you thought me cold—aloof.
And perhaps I was ... Now I'll give any proof
You ask that I adore you ... Oh my love! ...
See! On my knees I swear, by heaven above,
I'll weep, I'll beat myself, I'll tear my hair,
I'll starve, I'll kill myself in sheer despair
If you still doubt me—or if you're unkind!

AGNES: I see ... But love, I fear, 's both deaf and blind.
Even after that long speech my heart is chilled.
Yet with *two words* my lover would have filled
My soul with surging love for him ... For you
I'll *never* sigh—no matter what you do.

ARNOLPHE: Vixen! You goad me to the breaking point!
You witch, you'll be the death of me, aroint
You!... Out of town you'll go this very day!

                                     (*Agnes shrinks*)

A cloister cell is waiting. There you'll stay!

              (*Agnes flees. Enter Allan, hot and bothered*)

ALLAN: I don't know how it happened! ... You may
                                                    scoff ...

But Agnes and that corpse have just walked off!

ARNOLPHE: (*surly*)   She's here—imprisoned this time in
   my room!
Let her make love *there* with her precious groom
If he can reach her! ... I'll go find a carriage ...
With any luck she'll still be mine in marriage.
For when *she's* cloistered and *he's* out of sight,
Eventually the jade will see the light ...
Meantime, I charge you, guard her with your life!

ALLAN: I'll treat her just the way I'd treat my wife!

(*Exit Allan. Enter Horace, in extremis*)

HORACE: I've merely come to say farewell, my friend.
Your aid proved all in vain—this is the end!
Fate never dealt me such a blow as this...
They've come to put a stop to all our bliss!

ARNOLPHE: You've told me no less tragic tales before.
Who's "they?" ... I'm mystified ... Come, tell me more!

HORACE: My father ... I don't know where to begin....
My father's here ... in Paris ... at an inn!
With no pretence of even consulting me,
He's come to find some buxom wench that he
And Enrique, seemingly, have both selected
For me to wed ... You see why I'm dejected?
Why, when they told me, I did all but faint! ...
To reassure me they began to paint

A glowing picture of my future bride...
My ears refused to listen! ... I defied
Them both!

ARNOLPHE: You *are* a spirited young blade!

HORACE: Well, I *would* have ... had I not been afraid
To hear him give a flat and final *no*
To all my hopes of Agnes ... You must know
How much I love her!

ARNOLPHE: Yes, you've made that quite clear.

HORACE: Well, in five minutes they will both be here ...
For some strange reason they must talk with you.
So one sole thing remained for me to do:
Get here before they did and make appeal
To you! ... *Please*, come what may, do not reveal
Aught of my firm resolve to marry her—
Agnes, I mean. For if this should occur
We're doomed! ... Whereas, if granted some delay,
I'll find some means... Try, too, of course, I pray—
Since they respect your judgment—to dissuade
Them from obliging me to wed this maid!

ARNOLPHE: (*cheerful*)   *This* gives me food for thought,
I do declare!

HORACE: You stand alone between me and despair.

ARNOLPHE: (*gay*)   Well, you can count on me to try, my
friend!

HORACE: Right from the start I knew I could depend
On you!

ARNOLPHE: (*jubilant*)   And I've a feeling I'll succeed!

HORACE: So once again you'll prove a friend in need! ...
Why, here they are already....
(*He is greatly agitated*) Let's keep calm! ...
Tell them how very sensible I am ...
Tell them I'm far too young to marry! ...
They haven't an argument you cannot parry!

(*Enter Oronte, Chrysalde and Enrique*)

ENRIQUE: (*to Chrysalde*)   My wife's good brother! ....
Why, I'd have known you
Though I'd encountered you in Timbuctoo!
You have the same head—the same features fine—
The same gait—though, of course, more masculine! ...
Why did harsh death, while she was still a bride,
Snatch her so prematurely from my side! ...
I sigh to think how she'd have been delighted
To see the three of us this day united,
And her long-lost daughter wed to Oronte's son! ...
That is, if he consents to have this done?

ORONTE: Enrique, you don't require to hear my voice.
You know I could not make a wiser choice.

ARNOLPHE: (*to Horace*)   Now I see how—no, *what*—I'll
do for you!

HORACE: Take care!

ARNOLPHE: Don't worry! I'll await my cue!

ORONTE: (*to Arnolphe*)   I've longed for this embrace for
many a year!

ARNOLPHE: Judge, then, how glad I am to see *you* here!

ORONTE: I've come—

ARNOLPHE: No need to tell me—I know all.
Your son says he won't wed the maid you chose—
That much at least he's seen fit to disclose.
In fact, he has implored me not to rest
Until you have complied with his request
That he should wed some other—heaven knows
  whom!...
Ah, they're headstrong these gallants in the bloom
Of youth! ... That's why a father must be firm!
To be obeyed, you'll have to make him squirm!
This boy might quite well get it in his head
That *he*, not *you*, should pick the girl he'll wed!
In this he's far too young to have a say.
Wed him to Enrique's daughter! Don't delay!

HORACE: *Traitor!*

ORONTE: (*shaken*)   A father's wish is law, of course ...
Still, I would hate to marry him by force.
And I imagine Enrique would agree ...

ENRIQUE: Why, what seems good to you seems good to
  me.

ARNOLPHE: *I* was brought up to call the father fool
Who'd submit meekly to his children's rule!
I plead with you to take a stand this day!
It's now or never! ... Make your son obey!

ORONTE: (*swithering*) Perhaps you're right ...

ARNOLPHE: Think also of the shame
In which this breach of faith would plunge your name!

ORONTE: (*convinced*) Yes, now I *know* you're right ...
What's done is done.
I *wish* this marriage to take place, my son!

CHRYSALDE: (*to Arnolphe*) Try as I may, I can't quite
understand
Why *you* should advocate the marriage planned!
What is your motive? ... For you must have one.

ARNOLPHE: I do what's fit and proper to be done!

ORONTE: And you're right, dear Arnolphe!

CHRYSALDE: Arnolphe? For shame!
I've told you Monsieur de la Souche's the name.

ORONTE: No matter ...

HORACE: De la Souche? *What do I hear?*

ARNOLPHE: At last you find confusion growing clear! ...
The problem was a prickly one for me.

HORACE: I'm still aghast! ... So *you*, my friend, were
he!!!

(*Enter Georgette, on the run*)

GEORGETTE: I warn you, master, if you don't come fast,
That pretty lass may well have breathed her last!
She's at the window—and to hear her cries,
You'd think she'd jump out right before your eyes!

ARNOLPHE: Go fetch her!

GEORGETTE: She won't come!

ARNOLPHE: Then *drag* her down! ...
  Excuse my haste ... I must go out of town! ...
  (*to Horace*) Console yourself! Each has his turn, 'tis
    said.
  Too much good fortune goes to a man's head!

HORACE: I wonder whether, since the world began,
  Such anguish has been felt by mortal man!

ARNOLPHE: I said something like that—as I recall ...
  Well, good and bad luck come in turn to all! ...
  I'm off! (*to Oronte*) Meantime I urge you to prepare
  This marriage! ... You can count on *my* being there! ...

ORONTE: I can't conceive its happening without you.

  (*Enter Agnes, distraught—supported by Allan and Georgette*)

  So *you've* been making all this hullaballoo!

ARNOLPHE: Come, my rebellious beauty—show your
    face!
  Henceforth, perhaps, you'll learn to keep your place!
  Say farewell to your friend ... Curtsey once more—
  And for the last time! ... Yes, your hearts are sore—
  But best-laid schemes don't always come to pass! ...

AGNES: Don't let them take me, Horace!

HORACE: What, alas,
  With everyone against us, can I do?

ARNOLPHE: Off with you, baggage!

AGNES: No, I'll stay right here!!

ORONTE: Just what's going on is—I must say—unclear!

ARNOLPHE: Some day, when I've more time, I'll tell you all.
You'll learn what suffering held my heart in thrall!

ORONTE: But who's this girl? Where do you plan to go? ..
This much I'd like *right now* to know!

ARNOLPHE: All that's important I've already said ...
No matter how he feels—see that he's wed!

ORONTE: Remember this, then, before off you ride:
To get *him* wed, *you* must produce the bride!
For midst all this confusion, one thing's clear:
The girl my son will marry's living here!
The child, I mean, that my good friend Enrique
Had with Chrysalde's fair sister Angelique—
She's in your house!

(Arnolphe's final agony begins)

CHRYSALDE: My friend, you seem surprised!

ARNOLPHE: *(terrified)*   There's some mistake! ... I would
have been apprised ...
I don't believe it! ....

CHRYSALDE: Nonetheless, it's true!
When young Enrique came to our house to woo—

ENRIQUE: *His* sister was desired by a great duke.
But she loved *me*—and so refused to look
At him.

ORONTE: Thus both incurred the ducal wrath!

ENRIQUE: When we were wed, to throw him off our path,
We kept the marriage secret ...

CHRYSALDE: No one knew
They had a child, you see—not even you! ...

ORONTE: They sent her to the country to be raised
By a poor wench whose virtue they'd heard praised ...

CHRYSALDE: But the bad duke accused Enrique of theft,
And thus of his good name he was bereft ...

ENRIQUE: Leaving wife, daughter, I was forced to flee
To distant, barbarous lands beyond the sea ...

ORONTE: There he braved many perils! But at last
The ill luck that attended him was past.

CHRYSALDE: Riches were his! He basked in fortune's
smile!

ORONTE: Laden with gold, he traveled home in style!

CHRYSALDE: Meantime, alas, his wife had died of fever.

ENRIQUE: I cursed the day I was obliged to leave her!

CHRYSALDE: His one thought now was for that daughter
dear
On whom he'd not set eyes for many a year...

ORONTE: A patient search revealed the maiden's nurse
Had suffered from ill fortune even worse
Than he ...

CHRYSALDE: So poor she knew not what to do—
She was obliged to cede the child *to you*. ...

ENRIQUE: When she had reached the age of *four*.

ARNOLPHE: (*stricken*)   *No! No!*

ORONTE: Yes, yes! What he has said's exactly so!

ARNOLPHE: Agnes *can't* be his daughter!

ORONTE: Have no fear!
  Enrique has brought the peasant woman here.
  She'll know the child she cared for at a glance—
  Whate'er the time—place—circumstance!

ARNOLPHE: (*surrendering*) It must indeed be she ...

CHRYSALDE: You're quite upset,
  Of course... But things might have been much worse
      yet ...
  How fortunate your plan to wed her failed! ...
  If you still want to wed—you should be *jailed!*

ARNOLPHE: *I hate you all!*

                                        (*Exit*)

ORONTE: What an outburst of spite!

CHRYSALDE: By nature he's not harsh nor impolite
  Except when crossed on his pet subject—marriage!

HORACE: Darling, you're rid of him!

AGNES: There goes his carriage! (*And it does!*)

ORONTE: I feel this mystery would be crystal clear
  If we from one or both you could hear.

HORACE: There's really very little to explain—
  What poor Arnolphe has lost has been my gain! ...

The girl I said I simply couldn't see
Turns out to be the only girl for me!

AGNES: (*to Enrique*) If *you're* my father, I bring you a son—

For this day son and daughter will be one!
(*to Oronte*) I'll be a daughter, too, whom *you'll* approve, I trust!

ORONTE: And you and he will share my love!

CHRYSALDE: I'm sure I'm just as glad as any of you!
But my poor brain has had too much to do
With all these mysteries ... Let's go inside
And fill a brimming glass to toast the bride!

HORACE: (*tender but teasing*) *One* will at least be faithful to her man!

AGNES: (*archly*) I'll be at least as faithful as I can!